Barnaby and Me

"Behind Barnaby's bold-striped jacket, bow tie and straw skimmer is an autobiography with a wealth of good humor, funny adventures and enough dirty linen to dismay a less optimistic personality."
— *The Akron Beacon Journal*

"A revealing and hilarious look at [Sheldon's] career, which blossomed along with TV itself. The anecdotes are endless."
— *Sun Newspapers*

Linn Sheldon has no peer as a story-teller. Accordingly, *Barnaby and Me* is anything but a traditional biography. Rather, it is a series of true stories told by a master, and from those stories emerges a compelling portrait of a very complex and very, very funny man . . . Sheldon's stories and insights about early television and the people who pioneered the medium are as delightful as they are unique.
— *Ashtabula Star Beacon*

"An entertaining account of one of the more significant and enduring Northern Ohio TV pioneers."
— *Northern Ohio Live*

Barnaby *and* Me

Linn Sheldon
with Nat Howard

GRAY & COMPANY, PUBLISHERS
CLEVELAND

Photographs courtesy of the Cleveland Press
Collection, Cleveland State University Archives.

Gray & Company, Publishers
1588 E. 40th Street
Cleveland, Ohio 44103
www.grayco.com

ISBN 1-886228-42-6

Printed in the United States of America
First paperback printing

For my children,
Abby, Linda, and Perry,
and my wife, Laura

Contents

Foreword

For 32 years Linn Sheldon appeared on television as an elf named Barnaby and helped shape the lives of many thousands of children.

Grownups, too.

For *Barnaby* went where all too few shows would dare to go today: to the lifting of spirit; the wonderment of the times before us and beyond us; the joy of laughter; the blessings of freedom in a bountiful land; the great adventure of living.

Yet in all those years he never preached, never belittled, never berated, and never patronized. The young, the older, and the oldest who watched him all sensed the same thing: that Barnaby was a friend. That was the secret of Barnaby. From his first to last show, and within any given show, Linn Sheldon regarded his audience as one person, and he never let Barnaby forget that.

Because much of his career bloomed in the early days of live television, and because even when stations taped the shows they would keep tapes only a week or two before recording over them, there is very little footage of his shows. Too bad. They are in a class by themselves. Ask anyone who saw them.

Moreover, there are no written scripts, for in those 32 years Linn Sheldon never wrote a word for Barnaby. It was all ad-libbed.

There was a steamer trunk—one of those old, round-topped affairs with a big brass padlock—on Barnaby's TV set. The station crew, executives, other performers, and anyone else who felt like it would put things in there. An old hat. A magnifying glass. A telephone. A kazoo. A baby's bib. Whatever. If there were four or five minutes open at the end of the show, Barnaby would look inside and emerge with something he hadn't seen before, and fill the four or five minutes with it.

One time there was an empty birdcage in there, and voilà! the invisible parrot, Longjohn, was born; he would become a regular on the show.

Perhaps the most memorable scene Linn Sheldon ever did involved a lovely, translucent brown bottle. He used it to teach a simple but profound lesson: Any one kid by himself is great, but kids together are even more wonderful. To show this, Barnaby sang part of a song, in a child's voice, into the bottle, then capped it. The he sang the same words as a different child might sing it. Then a third voice, and a fourth, capping the bottle each time. Then he opened the bottle and out came the song, sung in perfect harmony by a barbershop quartet.

As it turns out, that's also a metaphor for his life. From the many stage and real-life roles he has played, out came the wonderful harmonies of the stories you are about to read.

It all comes naturally to him. The warm humor and melancholy grace that distinguished Barnaby clearly emerged from Sheldon's early life as a very lonesome kid in Norwalk, Ohio; hitchhiking across the nation and playing his banjo for his supper; being a star-struck teenager at the MGM studios in Hollywood; becoming a successful actor and stand-up comic; suffering in the alcoholic ward of a Cleveland hospital; being a flawed husband but fervent father; and being a friend.

Be sure of this: if Barnaby calls, we'll tell him we think he's the nicest person in the whole world.

—Nat Howard, Mike Olszewski,
Richard Osborne, Ed Walsh, editors

Barnaby
and Me

Introduction

For 32 years, I was a six-foot-tall elf named Barnaby. Though this is the role—if any—I will be remembered for, it was only one of many parts I played on television, in the legitimate theater, nightclubs, and, in a very minor way, the movies.

But nothing I did on stage or screen ever came close to the real-life script I've lived. I've been caught in a Texas tornado, trapped in quicksand, survived an airplane on fire, been accused of bank robbery, jolted in a two-car crash in a car wash, and done a stand-up comedy act at the point of a gangster's gun. When my mother died soon after I was born, I became, in effect, the illegitimate son of my legitimate father, and from the time I was seven years old I was on my own. I've been married to four absolutely beautiful ladies, have three spectacular children, and was in on the birth and the maturation of television. But while I have done everything I could ever dream of doing, I also stood helplessly by as my second wife died, and almost as helplessly by as the first and third divorced me. I drank away a good deal of my health, the love of some of the people I have loved the most, and most of the money I'd made in television, and that was a lot.

Laugh, clown, laugh. Right?

By contrast, Barnaby led a delightfully serene life. The world was his sweet apple, and his goal in life was simply to share it with anyone who happened to peek into a television set when he was around.

One of those he shared it with was me.

Thank Heaven for that. Who knows where I would have ended up had I not had Barnaby to fall back on. For no matter how badly I slipped, there was Barnaby insisting that I set aside my foibles du jour and pay attention to him and, of course, his thousands of friends in the audience.

And so I would, and be the better for it.

There was nothing schizophrenic about this. It was more like a writer whose characters start acting on their own. I could immerse myself in the role but was perfectly able to return to real life when the show was over.

That's not to say that Barnaby and I did not have a lot in common. Quite clearly, my loneliness as a child led to a pursuit of just about anything that would encourage others to like me, so when Barnaby finally showed up, it was as if he had been waiting in the wings all along, waiting for a cue from me to enter and breathe new life into a show that otherwise was headed for a quick demise.

So here are some stories about Barnaby and me. Every one of them is true, though I confess to an imperfect memory that might shift or shade a detail here and there. But Barnaby told me, just the other day, that that's okay.

"When I forget something, which is almost never," he said, "I like to think of it as autobiographic license. And if you think all those presidents and movie stars and sports heroes who wrote autobiographies remember everything exactly as it happened, then we need to talk."

Childhood

As I look back on my life, I see it as a kind of stage play—a comic opera, perhaps.

As the curtain rises we are in Puckerbrush, a crossroads about three miles east of a small town (just 3,000 people back then) called Norwalk, in Ohio. The year is 1920, and I have just had my first glimpse of the world. As I recall, it looked pretty interesting.

Soon after I was born my mother passed away. I'm told she was a very sweet woman, and one of the great sadnesses of my life is that I never heard her say, "I love you."

Nor could I have known that not many years later I would be set adrift in Norwalk—not through anyone's meanness, but through circumstance. But let me tell you, if you have to be alone, Norwalk is the place to be. The people there are kind and caring, and they will take turns feeding you and giving you a bed (or a couch, or a floor) to sleep on. They did that for me.

At the age of 12 or thereabouts, I go through a kind of middle age of childhood, and am taken in by a strange and wonderful family named Friend. There I teach myself how to play the banjo and the piano; am herded, rain or shine, to Sunday school; finish junior high school; enter high school; fall in love with almost every girl I see; and begin to realize that my destiny is hidden somewhere in the hazy world of show business.

So I pack my banjo, toothbrush, and an extra shirt, limber up my thumb, and hitch-hike to Florida in search of fame and fortune, to be sure, but mostly in search of myself.

1.

Puckerbrush is what they called the other side of the tracks. I was born in that poor section of Norwalk, in my grandparents' house. To say that I was not a planned baby is putting it mildly. I had two brothers and a sister, all poor, all much older and on their own in other towns by the time I came along. Our father, Harry Sheldon, was a gandy dancer on the Wheeling & Lake Erie Railroad. I know that his nickname was Peeny, but I have no idea why. He had abandoned the family some years before I was born, but whenever the W&LE sent him and his crew to lay track in the Norwalk district, he would get drunk and do his best to reestablish, if only for a night, what he perceived was his right of husbandry with my mother.

One such visit took place on a cold winter night, possibly Christmas of 1918. I know that because I was born on September 20, 1919, a year after the end of World War I.

* * *

Soon after I was born, my mother died.

My sister was there, and it was she who decided to name me Linn. I was named for the doctor who delivered me, George Finney Linn. On my birth certificate my father's name is listed as unknown. Apparently my sister's resentment for all our father had done to us was so strong she felt I might be better off if the world thought of me as an illegitimate child rather than the son of such a man.

Although I didn't realize it myself for many years, I was in the strange situation of being the illegitimate son of my own father.

But then, my life is full of strange situations.

* * *

I don't remember much about my mother's parents, Perry and Amy Richards, just little flashes of things. They had 11 children. My mother, Lena, was next to the youngest. I remember my aunts and uncles largely through a family picture. For a while I thought maybe they were a baseball team, because so many of them had beards, like the old House of David team.

I remember ducks and chickens, and riding a buckboard with my grandfather, and being in Council Bluffs, Iowa—although I haven't the faintest idea of how we got there or back, or what the purpose of the trip was.

When my grandfather died in 1926, my grandmother went to live with relatives in Detroit. No one, it seemed—none of their 11 children and not my brothers or sister—was in a financial or emotional position to care for an eight-year-old boy. It was a situation that must have caused some turmoil among them, for they were not unkind people. The upshot was that I would somehow have to fend for myself. I did that by hanging around, looking wistful and wan, until someone—an old neighbor, a friend of my mother's, the folks of a childhood pal—would say, "Okay, stay a few days."

When no one said that, I would sleep where I could—in doorways, on porch swings, in the back seats of cars that weren't locked. I learned very quickly how to beg for nickels so I could buy something to eat.

The idea of having to stay with different people for the rest of my life soon seemed perfectly normal to me, and not at all frightening. It turned out to be great basic training for the life of a vagabond.

Does all that sound unhappy? I don't mean it to.

You don't miss spaghetti if you've never had it.

* * *

So I became, in a sense, a child of the town, staying a few days or weeks in one house, then wandering off to another. Over the next year and a half several dozen Norwalk people took me in and fed and clothed me, for no better reason than that I would show up at their door, and they somehow felt obliged to do something about it. Only rarely did I not have a real bed, or at least the floor of a warm room, to sleep in. At times I had no choice but to sleep where I could, like the entrance to Citizen's Bank in downtown Norwalk, or under a tree in a park, or on a swing on someone's front porch.

The people who did take me in were wonderful. If they did so out of pity, I was never aware of it, perhaps because I myself never felt any reason to be pitied. It all seemed normal enough to me.

It was only later that I realized what sadness was there.

Sadness because I never heard "I love you."

Sadness because no one ever said to me, "Please don't go."

2.

When I was eight and full of wonder, kicking stones on the way home from school on an early summer day was as fine a way as any to pass the time. It was free time, a pause between the stuffiness of Mrs. Hildebrandt's classroom and the huffiness of grownups at home.

I kicked an awful lot of stones back then in Norwalk, Ohio, my hometown, and so did a lot of other kids dragging home from schools in thousands of towns like it across America. It was one of those unwritten codes of conduct for boys growing up in the 1920s, like making weird whistling noises by blowing hard on a blade of grass between your thumbs, or spitting through your two front teeth, or starting a club in the garage and taking on big-shot names like "Doc" and "Mush" and "Moose." (In my club, that was my name—Moose. I have no idea why. "Slats" or "Stick" would have been much more appropriate.) So I kicked stones and spat and assumed the name Moose for no better reason than I was eight years old and that's what eight-year-olds did in towns like Norwalk in the twenties. Another reason, no better than the first, was that school was going out and summer was coming in, and there wasn't a lot else to do.

So I'd kick my last stone of the day, open the screen door on our back porch, get a hug from my grandmother, and ask, "What's for supper?"

The answer, almost always, was: "Leftovers. And shut that door."

The memory of one particular meal comes back to me time and again. I don't remember what was said or what the leftovers were that evening. What I do remember, as clearly today as then, was a far-off humming sound that silenced all of us at the table—my grandmother, grandfather, and me—and the sense of wonder that filled the room. Without a word, I scrambled for the backyard with the grandfolks close behind.

"There it is!" someone shouted.

I was so small, and the sky so big, that even with everyone pointing it took me a while to see it. Then there it was: an airplane. A real airplane!

In a small town, in the twenties, the sight of a plane was still an awesome thing. We watched the miracle in the sky until it passed from sight, and watched the sky itself a good deal longer, hoping the plane would come back.

In bed that night, I flew that plane around the world a hundred times, sometimes upside down or backward or both, with an occasional loop thrown in for good measure.

* * *

Our town, along with its three thousand people, was surrounded by wheat fields, woods, and ponds alive with fish and small animals and birds you seldom see anymore—like flickers and bluebirds.

Saturday night was the big night of the week, and everyone would go "up town." The stores stayed open until nine o'clock. The ladies, their children in or almost in hand, would shop, and the men would stand around on the street corners talking, and sometimes I'd notice they'd move closer together and lower their voices, then slap their thighs and laugh. Being eight, I had no idea what they were whispering about, but now that I'm in my seventies, I'd be willing to bet a lot of money it had something to do with girls and hay.

The Saturday night after we'd seen the plane, my grandmother and I were going into the dime store on East Main Street and saw in the window a big cardboard poster with a picture of a beautiful red biplane on it. The plane and its two pilots, it announced, would land at the Whitney farm a week from Sunday, and anyone lucky enough to have a dollar would be given the ride of his or her life.

I didn't have a dollar or any idea how to get one, but I made up my mind right then and there I was going for a ride in that airplane.

Ever since children were invented, they have promised God many things for many reasons. In my prayers that week, I promised Him that if I could have just one ride and come back to earth safely, He'd have no more trouble with me. Never. Ever. Amen.

* * *

No matter how hard you try to hurry it up, each day must pass before the next one comes. In my sight that week, a moment gone was but a thousand ages. But, finally, the wait was over, and I stood on the field at the Whitney farm under a beautiful blue Sunday-morning sky. I still remember the stubble on the field, and how dry it was for lack of rain. I paced back and forth wondering how all those people could sit still in those cars parked along the roadside, just waiting.

Pretty soon, things started to happen. A gasoline truck pulled up to the curb at the edge of the field, and some men got out of their cars and talked to the driver. Kids were running around, excited like me. Voices got louder as the crowd grew larger and speculation built up. People were pointing in all directions. Someone pushed someone else, and threats were muttered. It was hot and getting more humid by the moment and the crowd was beginning to tap its foot, so to speak, in anticipation of what would soon come.

A black dot against the blue of the sky, and a hush fell over the crowd. Slowly, the dot took on the shape of a biplane, and the black gave way to bright red. Then we could make out the silhouette of the pilots, one behind the other, and then little flutters of white from the silk scarves around their necks. They circled the field and landed. The motor sputtered to a stop, and the two men climbed out of the open cockpits. Not mere men, mind you, but all my heroes—Babe Ruth, Ty Cobb, Red Grange, Casey Jones—rolled into two guys named "Cap" and "Ace." I got caught up in the crowd, but by crawling under and over, in between and around, I came face to face with them. Looking up, I could see their flight helmets, goggles, leather jackets, and scarves.

Even I knew you couldn't fly an airplane without wearing a white silk scarf.

They got right down to business. Cap would collect the money, and Ace would fly the plane. Everything seemed ready until the guy with the truck refused to carry the cans of gas from the truck to the plane.

"I'll carry it!" I shouted.

Cap looked down at me, patted my head, and said,

"Thanks, kid, but that can will have to be carried back and forth all day, and I don't think you're big enough for the job."

"I can do it. I know I can. Let me try . . .," I pleaded.

He grinned and said—I know he said it—"Kid, you got the job, and I'll tell you what. You work all day, and before we leave, Ace and I'll give you a free ride."

For a free ride, I'd have carried the truck back and forth.

* * *

Excitement always makes time pass quickly, but now it was setting new speed records. I carried that can back and forth, and I didn't tire. Just the thought of flying turned the can to feathers.

Being that close to the action, I was able to pick up bits and pieces of pilot talk and made a point of dropping a few of them within earshot of the kids I passed while hauling the cans of gas.

"Prop's working about right," I'd murmur. Or: "Great struts!" And the big one: "Those ailerons are the best I've ever seen."

As the sun set on the far end of that hot, dry field, the crowd thinned out, and cars headed home.

My time had come.

Ace and Cap, by now my squadron mates, were talking at the tail end of the plane. Ace reached over and grabbed the rudder, moving it right, then left and right again. He frowned and made a *tch tch* sound with his tongue. He said something to Cap, but I couldn't make it out.

Cap called me over and put his hand on my shoulder.

"Kid," said Cap, "There may be a problem with the

tail assembly. Ace and I'll run her down the field and back and check it out. We don't want to put you in any danger. It'll only take a minute." As they got into their seats, I hollered up, "I'm still going up, right?" "Sure, kid, sure," Cap yelled back. "We wouldn't forget you."

Slowly, the plane lumbered down the field, turned into the wind, and picked up speed. Then it lifted off the ground and banked to the right.

"Good," I said to myself. "She's working fine." I could hardly wait.

Instead of circling the field, that beautiful red biplane climbed higher and higher, and got smaller and smaller. They were gone. The moment became so heavy within me that I could no longer look up.

* * *

That Sunday morning so long ago a little boy walked onto that field. A young man walked off.

3.

My grandfather drank a lot of home brew, dandelion wine and hard cider, right out of the jug. I was living with my grandparents on the farm in Puckerbrush. It was a typical farm for that time and place . . . some chickens, a few pigs, a couple of cows. The plow was a single-blade wheelbarrow plow pulled by a mule, the reins around my grandfather's shoulders.

Walking behind that plow for hours every day was hard, grueling, dull work, except when you were plowing along the north side of the farm, next to a country road. Then, at least, people were likely to come by and wave.

Those passersby could tell when my grandfather was drinking, which was usually, because the furrows in the field would be crooked. When it got worse than that—like the time he plowed diagonally across the field, got halfway to the other side, turned 90 degrees, and headed toward the corner—he would instruct me to tell my grandmother that the mule was acting up again and wouldn't go where he told him to go. He didn't mention that the mule was pulling both the plow and a man who had just gone through about three quarts of hard cider.

One day a man came to our house with a bunch of papers for my grandfather to read and sign. It seems a distant cousin in England named William Saybrook had passed on, and grandfather was the only heir to his estate, whatever that may prove to be.

To say that Grandfather was excited is putting too fine

a point on it. We had never met the man, but grandfather had always referred to him as Lord Saybrook, and it was presumed that he had a substantial estate.

Some time later the man returned with the inheritance. It was a check for something in the neighborhood of 25 bucks along with a few pictures and family artifacts and a fine top hat, striped pants, gray vest, and black tailcoat.

My grandfather didn't know what to do. When he first got wind that there would be some inheritance he bumped his drinking up a notch and told anyone who would listen that he was going to sell the farm, travel around the world, buy fine things, and dress like the gentleman he knew himself to be. Now that dream was shattered.

Well, most of it.

A few days later, we heard a crash along the roadside, and ran out to see what it was. A man in a horse and buggy had run off the road and into a tree on our property. His buggy was a mess, but he was not seriously hurt.

He told us he had been distracted by the man behind the mule over there, plowing the field.

We turned and saw grandfather behind the plow, resplendent in black tailcoat, gray vest, striped pants, everything but the top hat. He was singing a song from his childhood. Nearby, in one of the furrows, was an empty jug.

The hat was on the mule.

4.

The house at 17 State Street in Norwalk was the closest thing to a real home I would know as a child. Bill and Theo and Julia Friend were brothers and sister, and I lived in their home more or less regularly from the time I was eight until shortly after I turned 15, when I packed up my banjo and struck out on my own.

The Friends were moderately wealthy, highly cultured, and very weird.

Theo was the weirdest. All I really knew about him was that he had written a book on electricity and matter, and lived as a recluse on the third floor.

Bill and Julia were very big on music, the Episcopal church, righteousness, and eating the right things. Smoking and drinking were terrible sins, and it was made clear to me that I would be punished if I ever so much as talked to a drunk.

In fact, it was so important to Bill that I sing in the choir at the Episcopal Church that he gave me a penny to do so—pretty good money for a kid of eight in 1927. And almost every Sunday he would find me guilty for some real or imagined trespass, and take the penny back as punishment.

One Sunday after church he saw me talking with a man who was very drunk.

He made me give back the penny he had given me before church, and vow again to never talk to a drunk.

He knew the man I had been talking to, and so did I. It was my father.

* * *

Jane Berkley, a lovely black lady who for some reason called me "Lindbergh," did the cooking and the cleaning in the Friends' big home.

There was a bird feeder just outside one of the windows in the music room. When squirrels would raid the feeder for sunflower seeds, Jane would feed them walnuts; she actually trained two of them—"Foxie" and "Loxie," she called them—to sit on her shoulders.

I loved that, and I loved her, but I worried that the squirrels might pick at my banjo, or jump on my guitar or the piano, for I had by then developed a passion for music and musical instruments. That passion was nourished by Bill and Julia Friend's own love of music. They each played the piano often and well.

Theo, the brother who lived on the third floor, was apparently a kind of mad genius. He never ate with us. In fact, we probably didn't see him more than three or four times a year. I was told that when Theo got a cold he would wear only his winter underwear—longjohns with a flap in the rear—and old sheepskin slippers. Then he would put a paper bag, with holes cut out for eyes and mouth, over his head, and chew on a long, black licorice stick.

* * *

I was about 12 or 13, and had begun to suspect that girls might actually be more interesting than, say, frogs or jackknives. In fact, I was now thinking a lot more about girls than just about any other subject.

There was Mary across the street, Hilda down the block, and any other girl that happened by. But it was Alice, in particular, who gave rise to dreams of glory. Oh, how I liked Alice! She was my age. She was pretty. She was very healthy, I noticed, and she went to the same beautiful and cavernous Episcopal church that I attended.

Once I asked Julia if I could bring Alice home after church for Sunday dinner, the kind of Sunday dinner that seems to have vanished from America along with letter writing, street baseball, and a whole lot more.

The next Sunday was cold and wet, so we walked home as fast as we could. Inside, I took her coat and turned to hang it on the hall coat tree. When I turned back Alice was staring upward, her face pale, eyes wide.

I looked up. At the top of the stairs sat Theo, resplendent in his double-hung longjohns and sheepskin shoes, with a black licorice stick protruding through the mouth hole of the bag over his head.

Alice was getting ready to run, I sensed, so I hustled her into the music room, turned back to the hall, and said to Theo, "Please, sir, go back upstairs." He muttered something and went back into the attic.

I walked back into the music room and saw Alice, eyes wide open, jaw agape, staring at Jane Berkley, who stood by the window, a squirrel on each shoulder.

That was the day I learned that ladies sometimes get headaches.

5.

Harvey Cooper was a teacher in our school, but he had, it seemed to me, an even higher calling: to strike terror into the heart of any young boy who dared so much as think about S-E-X.

I was 14, and like every other 14-year-old boy I had already done a considerable amount of wondering and worrying about sex. I really didn't need Harvey Cooper or anyone else to make it any scarier.

But we had no choice. Attendance was required at his little after-school seminar on sex, presumably on the premise that if we heard it from a respectable grownup like Mr. Cooper we'd get it right—not all mixed up like we would if we heard about it from some other kid who'd already done it.

Here—no kidding—is what Harvey Cooper told us:

1. A man can only have sex 100 times. Not once more.

2. What the body expels in an orgasm is in fact gray matter from the brain. Thus every time you have sex, you get a little dumber: do it 50 times and you'll be only half as smart as you were when you started out. The closer you get to zero, the dumber you get.

3. The chances of getting some terrible disease from any kind of sex are pretty close to 100 percent.

Part of me said it might be a good idea never to go near a girl again. Maybe don't even take a warm bath again. But even though I hadn't lost any gray matter yet, I somehow knew I was destined to become a very stupid person.

Harvey Cooper's warnings were keeping perfect time with my pounding pulse when some months later I moseyed into a toolshed with a girl named Rosie who, it was said, "had been around." She was much older than I, in her twenties. She sat down on a bale of hay and raised her skirt and one eyebrow as if to ask, "Okay, buster, whaddaya going to do about that?"

I thought: "I'm at 100 percent now and I'm pretty smart. Who's going to notice if I drop down to 99?"

I did what had to be done.

It didn't take long at all for the million pins to hit me. What I hadn't realized was that at that same wonderful moment she accidentally kicked a rake that was leaning against the wall of the toolshed. It fell over and hit me in the head.

I said to myself, sex from the waist down is great.

But when the gray matter leaves your brain, that really hurts.

* * *

For the next few weeks my thoughts shifted between the delights of my encounter with Rosie and the horrors, so vividly detailed by Harvey Cooper, that would surely follow. But nothing happened: no rash, no blindness, no limbs dropping off. Finally, I screwed up my courage and went to see Dr. Linn, the man who brought me into the world and for whom I was named. I told him everything—what Harvey Cooper had said about every man getting only 100 shots at it, and what Rosie and I had done, and how scared I was.

He assured me that there is no known limit to the number of times a man can reach a climax, and it has nothing to do with intelligence.

When I left his office, it was all I could do to keep from running up and down the street yelling "Rosie! . . . Rosie! . . . Where are you, Rosie . . ."

6.

Looking into a mirror at any age is an adventure that seldom comes out the way it goes in.
Your ego says one thing, the looking glass another. I felt I was six foot two. The mirror showed five foot eight, and the 186 pounds of muscle and courage came back as 124 pounds of limp chicken.

But what can you expect when you're 15 and had slept through puberty, dreaming of hunting ducks? Still I know, somehow, that tonight my life will change forever. I have my first date. Not with just any girl, but the prettiest and smartest girl in the world.

I say smartest, for she said "Yes," while the others said "No."

The plan for the evening went something like this . . . first to the school dance, then on to the Candy Kitchen for a soda, and finally a starlit stroll to her house, the one with the swing on the front porch.

Getting ready for the big moment took on a kind of religious fervor, like a bullfighter before his last great fight. First the bath, then lots of talcum over and under everything. I plastered enough goo on my hair to be a fire hazard. Next, on with the clean BVDs and into my tweed pants, known to my family as "the other pair." On with the socks, both the same color, and then on with the shoes, but not my own. They looked terrible, and the left sole had worked loose and made a flapping sound when I walked, so I borrowed my stepbrother's shoes. He used the word "swiped" later.

The shoes were size 10, and I wore a 7. A wad of paper in each toe did the trick, otherwise I might have danced all night in shoes that never moved.

Now the shirt, still smelling a little of Fels Naptha soap, topped off with a nifty bow tie. The last bit of hand-me-down elegance was a black sport coat with only one gravy stain you'd have to really look for to see.

A final look in the mirror, and this time it seemed to say, "Look out, world, a lover is loose!"

* * *

Her name was Annie, and she lived two streets over from our house, so I cut across lots to save time. Finally I was standing at her door. My heart was up to about 90 miles an hour as I checked my hair, shoes, and each button from fly to tie. Then I raised my arm, said "here goes," and rapped on the door.

Her mother opened it and invited me in. I thanked her and stumbled into the parlor. I was so scared I couldn't think of anything to say. I just sat there, trying my best to look nonchalant.

And then . . . there was Annie.

Oh, my, she was pretty! When she said, "Hi," all I could say, like Tonto, was "We go now." As we were leaving, a voice from the kitchen, her father's, boomed: "Remember, ten o'clock," and at last we were going down the steps and into a beautiful memory.

* * *

Annie set a fast pace going up State Street, but I showed her I could walk just as quickly sideways, then backward, even in my stepbrother's shoes. I don't have the slightest memory of what we talked about, but I do know it was the best conversation I've ever forgotten.

We arrived at the dance, our tickets in my left hand, 20 cents in my pocket, and the world's most beautiful girl beside me. Could any man wish for more?

All of us have great expectations, the kind that will be fulfilled at a special time called "someday." The music began, and as I turned and took Annie's hand in mine, the dawn of my own "someday" arrived. We danced, laughed, and talked with friends until the band played "Good Night, Sweetheart" and it was time to go.

Our hearts were sweet, to be sure, but we weren't ready for the "good night" part.

* * *

It was a time in our century when no matter where you lived there was a place where everyone went after the dance. In my town, Norwalk, Ohio, that place was called the Candy Kitchen. It had other names in other towns, but they were all very much alike and they all had the same ultimate reason for being: that the night must never end.

The specialty of our hangout was the 10-cent choco- late soda. Over the din of voices, pitched somewhere between loud and call the cops, the waitress somehow heard my order for two sodas, and when they came we dug in and didn't come up for air till we'd finished lick- ing the spoons. Then Annie said something that made me wish I were at least dead.

"Can we have another?"

Looking down at the table, too embarrassed to look her in the eye, I said as quietly as possible, "I don't have any money."

"What?" she asked, leaning over so close I could smell her perfume, even in that noisy crowd.

I swallowed what little pride I had left and said, only this time so she could hear, "I'm out of money."

"That's all right," she said, "we can have another next time."

My mind went reeling. Next time? Wow . . . there was going to be a next time!

* * *

Walking home was slow and easy. A moon fell out of a song and followed us at every turn. We talked about what we liked and didn't like and when the next time would be. And when I walked sideways and backward, so did she.

All too soon we reached her house. Her folks were on the porch, sitting in the wicker chairs. Her father had his feet up on the railing, and her mom said, "Come sit on the swing and tell us about the dance." We did.

The swing was made of wood, and it hung from the porch ceiling by heavy chains at each end. Its motion was gentle, and its squeak somehow spoke of summer.

Her father yawned and said, "Well, I have to get up early, so I'd better be getting to bed." Just as I was about to say good night, her mother told us we could sit for a few minutes while she finished up inside.

Annie and I were alone, and only 15, but the swing was old and seemed to slow down by itself and stay silent, as if to help us listen to the music of the night. The katy-dids were all in tune, joining the breeze and the leaves in a strange and wonderful song. Even the distant whistle of the night mail train on the Wheeling and Lake Erie chimed in.

All too soon, from inside, came the words, "It's time."

We went to the door, said our good nights and thank you's, and I walked back to 17 State Street, but my feet never touched the ground.

A few weeks later, Annie and her family moved away from Norwalk, and I never got a second date with her.

But that first one was so sweet I can taste it still.

7.

Live Bait

Now a minnow is delicious
For any fish who wishes
To end up as a story on a wall.
But to catch the angler's winner,
For a trophy or a dinner,
The humble little worm is best of all.
Although it's very easy,
Some find it slightly queasy,
To place this tasty tidbit on the line.
But to bass or speckled trout
It's what living's all about.
They'll hook it to their lips every time.
Now if someone comes in sight
Who's a fishing neophyte,
Be nice and tell him
What and where and why.
Then throw your fish'n pole
In your favorite fish'n hole,
Buy a fish and tell a whopp'n lie!

— Linn Richard Sheldon, 8th Grade, Miss Mossman

Although the school day was over, I was still seated in
Miss Mossman's eighth-grade English class. The other
students were walking out and probably wondering, as

I was, why she told me to stay. I hadn't said *ain't* all day, and I'd gotten a "C" on my poem, "Live Bait." So why me?

She kept fooling with some papers, writing notes here and there. I screwed up my nerve and said, "You wanted to speak with me, Miss Mossman?"

"Oh, yes—I'm sorry. Whenever I grade papers I forget other things, and time does fly. Now. Have you ever been in a play?"

"No," I said. "The only thing like that I've ever done was reciting my poem on 'Live Bait.'" I didn't tell her I thought it deserved at least a "B".

"Well, it doesn't matter," she said. "I think you'd do very nicely as the lead character in the spring play. Would you like that?"

Would I like it? I didn't know much about plays, but I was sure the lead was the guy who had the most to say and, better yet, got to kiss all the girls. They say when you're drowning your life passes in front of you. My shoes weren't even wet, but now my life started passing by—not the one I'd lived so far, but the one I was going to live as a movie star.

I could see it all. I'd do the play, and my picture would be in the paper. Then some big Hollywood producer would see it and say, "Get him." Sure, I knew I was a little on the skinny side, had asthma and buckteeth, but with makeup, who knows?

"Well?" asked Miss Mossman. "Do you want to give it a try?"

"Yes Ma'am," I said. Who wouldn't want to play the hero who catches the bad guy and gets the girl?

As if she read my thoughts, she smiled and said, " I'm

afraid it's not a very romantic part. It's about Frederic Chopin, the composer, dying of tuberculosis. I think you'd make a perfect Chopin."

I swallowed hard. Me—Mr. Asthma—a 97-pound Chopin wheezing to death in front of an audience. Well, why not? My new career had to start somewhere, so I said, "I'll be glad to play Chopin, and if you like, I'll get my Aunt Helen to teach me a few tunes on the accordion."

She turned that idea down.

* * *

We rehearsed the play every day after school for the next three weeks, using the classroom as a stage. Chairs, bookcases, hall trees, and other furnishings served as doors and windows and props, and Miss Mossman's desk as the piano. I would sit at the desk and run my hands up and down the imaginary keyboard, like Chopin in top form. On the night of the play, the plan was for me to sit at a real piano onstage and pretend like mad, while Miss Mossman was making Chopin a little sicker backstage.

No one would be the wiser, I was sure.

By the second week, I had my lines and coughs down about right. But one thing kept bothering me. Her name was Pearl, and she was in the play, too.

I'd known girls all my life, and I knew about the birds and the bees. But Pearl wasn't just any girl, and certainly neither bird nor bee.

Pearl was a thunderstorm, and I was a desert desperate for rain.

Rehearsals went on, and the one-night performance was getting close, but outside the play I was getting no closer to Pearl. Did I like her? Oh, yes! Did she like me?

I didn't know! What should I do? I didn't know that either.

Maybe I should just walk up to her and say: "Hi. I'm Frederic Chopin and I'm going to die soon, so could I have a date before I go?"

Maybe I'd get a laugh and the spell would be broken, but I couldn't get past "Hello."

* * *

The big night came and things were going well until I sat down to fake the first piano number. I finished and stood up, but Miss Mossman was still playing away in the wings.

It happened a second time, and the show slowly became "Chopin and His Magic Piano."

* * *

When the curtain came down, for it had no other place to go, the moms and dads, teachers and friends of the school applauded politely—not loud, but distinctly polite. Then they came backstage like there was going to be free food, milled around, and told each and every one of us how great we were.

One guy wanted to know where he could get a piano like that.

Another told me my makeup made me look as if I was really dying. Who should know better? He was the town's undertaker.

I wasn't wearing any makeup.

* * *

All of us in the play stood around as if nothing like

this would ever happen again. Some hoped it wouldn't; some wanted to do it again. But all I wanted to do was find Pearl. I wandered around and then just stood still. Where was she? Then bump. I turned, and there she was. I put out my hand, she took it, and I said, "Wonderful."

I didn't mean the play, I meant the moment; it was something that even all these years later would be "once upon a time." She said, "Thank you," and walked away.

I'd known the joy of Christmas, the glee that came with the last day of school, the excitement of a bobber jumping on the surface of a pond, the wonder of a shooting star. But until then, I had not known love.

* * *

Barney Evert was the school's football and basketball star, the captain of captains. The word was that he'd "been around" (wink, wink!), and it was not unusual to see him zipping all around town in his folks' new Hudson. Put him in a potato sack, and the girls would say, "Wow! Does he look great in that potato sack!"

Now Barney and I were only sort of friends, but when it came to basketball he and I had something in common. During the games he wore my tennis shoes.

So why not tell him about Pearl? With the weight of his experience and the power of my hope, we just might be able to solve my problem.

Barney had an idea . . . a frightening one, but I was ready to try anything. He'd give Pearl a call and tell her about the new Hudson, and how beautiful it was inside and how fast it could go. Then he'd ask if she'd like to go for a ride. If she said yes, the rest of the plan was easy.

Easy for him.

The idea was for me to get in the trunk of the car. Then he'd pick up Pearl, and while they were riding around he'd bring up the subject of his old pal, Chopin, and ask her what she thought of him. Curled up with the Firestone tire in the trunk, I'd be able to hear every word. If she said she was crazy about me, he stops the car, lets me out of the trunk, and we'd live happily ever after.

He called, and she said she'd love to go for a ride in his car. I fairly leaped into the trunk, I was so excited. It was a little crowded what with the tire, the jack, Barney's dad's hip boots. But for love—anything.

"Be sure to talk loud," I said as he closed the trunk. "And make it fast. It's not exactly comfortable in here."

When you're in the trunk of a moving car and it's very dark, you find yourself considering things you'd never thought of before, like, what if there's a rear-end collision? And if there was, and even if you weren't hurt, how would you explain your presence there to the cops? Then you become aware that, from the inside, trunks have a distinct odor—like jungle rot. Then you wonder, is it the trunk or is it me?

Put it this way. The longer we drove, the less convinced I was that this was the smartest way to find out if a girl liked me.

Barney yelled, "We're almost there. I can see her now—she's on the porch." He stopped the car and said, "Here goes!"

It became very quiet, and the temperature rose to somewhere around medium rare. The door opened and I heard some chatter between Barney and Pearl as they got into the car.

Then it was off for a ride no amusement park ever offered. Barney and Pearl were both talking, but not loud enough for me to make out what they were saying. Then it got bumpy, like we were on a dirt road outside of town. All of a sudden we made a quick stop, and Barney turned off the motor. Then Pearl spoke.

"I love the reservoir this time of day. The sunset is so beautiful on the water."

The reservoir. The place where lovers go to talk a little and love a lot.

Barney and Pearl talked very little, and then not at all. Then the car began to move again, but it wasn't like before. It was a steady, rocking motion, and the motor wasn't running.

* * *

When it finally dawned on me what was happening, it hurt so bad I started to cry—quietly, of course. The harder I tried to block out a mental picture of what must be happening up front, the less successful I was.

There was a long silence and, finally, the car started up again, moving the way a car is supposed to move.

On the way back, I really kicked the shit out of that Firestone tire.

Florida, Hollywood, and World War II

At the age of 15 I have pretty much convinced myself that the only real skill I possess is entertaining others; therefore, show business must be the life for me. But first I wrestle momentarily with the problem of having to pay for food or die, so I do the right thing and take a job that includes escorting old ladies in their wheelchairs around St. Petersburg, Florida.

I leave Florida and head west, not at all sure what lies ahead. While I am working at a lodge on the south rim of the Grand Canyon, a very famous person whose name means nothing to me hears me play the banjo, is impressed, and invites me to look him up if I ever get to Hollywood.

Some months and a lot of hitchhiking later I am in Hollywood. I come across the card of the man who spoke to me at the Grand Canyon, find a pay phone, and call him up. He invites me to his workplace: the MGM studios.

I am hired as a kind of intern/gofer at MGM and meet many of the world's legendary movie stars. Spencer Tracy says "Hi," Hedy Lamarr gives me a kiss, and I get arrested for bank robbery.

In spite of my best efforts, World War II breaks out, and since I am now 18 and reasonably healthy I am invited to serve the U.S. army—or else.

8.

I hitchhiked to California by way of Florida.
At the time I thought Florida was my destiny, since it was a kind of retirement mecca for the wealthy people in Norwalk, Ohio. For as long as I could remember I had heard people talk about how beautiful the ocean beaches and the palm trees were, and what a fantastic sport deep-sea fishing was.

I could hardly wait to retire.

In fact, as I turned 15, I decided I would retire from high school and find my future and fortune in the sun-kissed state.

After all, I had a thumb and a banjo, so I knew I could travel free by hitchhiking, and with my banjo I could, as the old song went, sing for my supper.

So I greased up my thumb, put my banjo, along with an extra pair of socks and another shirt, in its case and headed south.

No sane person today would dream of hitchhiking that far, but in those days it was commonplace. People really did trust each other a lot more back then. That's not to say it was all that comfortable. There were no high-speed freeways then, and cars were bumpy, noisy, and hot—air conditioning was a comfort of the future. Still, since it didn't exist, we didn't really miss it that much.

On the way down I would find a roadside tavern or some other watering hole and ask if I could play my banjo. If they said yes, which they usually did, I would play songs like "Wait Till the Sun Shines, Nellie," "You Wore a Tulip," "Back Home in Indiana," and some of the folks would sing along.

I would pass my hat, and most of the time would get the 15 or 20 cents I'd need for a bed for the night. Sometimes I would sleep free at a Salvation Army hostelry or a City Mission.

I was, of course, very young, and not at all strong. I weighed 89 pounds—and that's with the banjo, *ta dum*. To make sure no one would swipe them I would tie my shoes together with their laces. I also had a very long belt, and when I went to bed (usually little more than a mattress in a mission-type dormitory) I would put my banjo on my chest and wrap the belt around it and me.

As far as I know, no one ever tried to steal anything from me.

For a nickel, you could sometimes get something to eat in the morning—a doughnut and coffee, maybe. If you looked forlorn enough—and I could look more forlorn than anyone I know—you might even get that for free.

I enjoyed that trip thoroughly. I was certainly as free as anyone in the world could be, and, as I look back on it, freer than at any other time of my life. As a rule, people would stop and say, "Where're you going?" You'd say, "Down the road," and they would say "All right, I'm going about 50 miles," and they'd drop you off maybe 40 or 60 miles later.

One day three guys pulled up in an old Studebaker. They had spotted my banjo case and reasoned that if there wasn't a Tommy gun in there it had to be a banjo.

"Hey, kid," one of them asked, "can you sing melody?"

I said sure I can. So they picked out a tune, and I had to stand by the car, play the banjo, and sing with them.

I was auditioning for a ride.

What they were was three parts of a barbershop quartet, and as long as I sung melody and played the banjo I could ride as far as they were going, which was a very nice, long stretch indeed.

When I finally reached Miami it was very late at night and it was raining. I found a park bench under a palm tree, curled up as best I could and went to sleep. When morning came the rain had stopped, the sun was glorious, and it was even more beautiful than I had imagined.

I walked along Miami Beach and marveled at the great hotels that had sprung up there. One of them was called the Traymore. I went in the employees' entrance. I don't remember what I said, but they must have been hard up, because I got a job as a bellhop.

But bellhopping was not for me, I soon decided. I kept looking at all those elegantly dressed people, thinking, I want to be like that, and how can you be like that if you're a bellhop?

To make matters worse, I weighed less than some of the luggage they had me carry.

So I asked around about other jobs and ran into a guy who said he had a brother who was the manager of a hotel in St. Petersburg called the Dusenberry. He told me I could go there and get a job—just mention his name.

I quit my bellhop job, got out my old banjo case, and hitchhiked to St. Petersburg. As I walked down its streets, I noticed a lot of ramps—ramps all over the place—for old people with canes and wheelchairs. The prospects did not look very exciting.

I kept asking for directions to the Dusenberry Hotel, but no one seemed to have heard of it. Finally some-one said, "Do you mean the Dusenberry Old Ladies' Home?"

Oh, no, I thought. But oh, yes, it was true. I found the place, and it had a bell-shaped porch with about 50 white rocking chairs on it.

I went in and everyone said, "Hello there, young man . . ."

I went to the manager's office and dropped the name of the guy from the Traymore. All it got was a blank stare. I told him I needed work, and he allowed as how they could use someone to run the elevators in the day and set up the card tables in the evening. For that I would get $3 a week and a room in the back with a cot.

Well, I wasn't planning on going anywhere else, so that sounded pretty good to me.

The elevator was something else. It was all manual, of course. You stepped in, pulled an old screen door across, then slowly and gently turned a handle right or left, and the elevator would go slowly up or down. If you pulled the handle way over, it would go faster. If you let it go it would snap back to the middle, and the elevator would stop with a bang.

I got to know many of the ladies there. They were very nice to me, but it was difficult living on nickel and dime tips and waiting for the three bucks pay at the end of the week.

I saved money by eating in the restaurant across the street. It was called the Triangle Restaurant, and for a dime they would put in front of me the highest stack of buckwheat cakes I had ever seen. I'd go in, order a stack,

and eat every bit of it. At noon I would drink a lot of water, my stomach would swell up, and I'd kid myself that
I'd had another big meal.

In fact, people started calling me "Buckwheat."

My excitement over Florida began to pale consider-
ably, and I began to think that maybe my destiny was
not there, but in California. But I really didn't believe I
would ever be able to make enough money to go there.

Then fate stepped in, in the form of a very sweet lady
named Miss Darling.

Miss Darling was pushing 70, and also pushing about
180 pounds. She walked with a cane, poor thing, and
had weak kidneys, and when she got on the elevator she
would always say, "Young man, take it up slowly. Stop
this thing gently." And others would warn me that if I
stopped too suddenly, poor Miss Darling would have an
accident of the unmentionable sort.

One day she said to me: "Young man, you have
Wednesdays off, don't you?" I said yes, and she said,
"How would you like to push me in a wheelchair around
St. Pete's?" I said fine. I figured that shoving someone
who outweighed me by plenty around the city would be
worth at least five bucks, and that was big money. California, here I come!

So Wednesday came, and I went to her third-floor
quarters. I helped her into the wheelchair (slowly),
wheeled her to the elevator (slowly), and took her down
(slowly).

I brought it and her to a gentle stop, then wheeled her
to the ramp, down the ramp, and onto the street. This
was in June, and it was about 190 degrees—in the shade.
Centigrade. She was dressed in all her finery, but some-

how managed to look cool. She waved like royalty at everyone we passed, while I huffed and puffed under the weight and the heat.

She said she wanted to go to Webb's Drug Store. In those days, Webb's boasted magnificent window displays and was said to be the biggest drugstore in the world. We went up and down every aisle in the store. There were fans, but no air conditioning.

Then it was back past the Dusenberry and into the department stores. Slowly up the elevator and slowly back down.

She wanted to go to the library. My huffing and puffing getting ever more substantial.

Bless her heart, she had made some sandwiches for lunch, and I got a little rest as we sat and watched old folks play shuffleboard. We had no lemonade, but she had a tin cup and I filled it at a nearby fountain. Later in the afternoon we watched some old people playing baseball, and it was fun. She bought me a hot dog there.

But it was still very hot, and she was very heavy—up to about 400 pounds, I figured, by the time we got back to the Dusenberry.

Back on the elevator. To the third floor, slowly. Stop, gently. We got to her room, and I'm about ready to faint from exhaustion, but the image of the five-dollar tip kept me going.

She said, "Young man, come up and see me after dinner, and I will give you something that will make you realize that today was really worth while."

Oh boy, I thought, maybe it would be six bucks . . . even seven.

After dinner I hurried back to her room. She said

"Close your eyes and hold out your hand." I shut my eyes and she placed a bunch of paper in my hands, but it wasn't dollars. It was her personal stationery, and on each sheet was a poem she had made up about Florida, alligators, and St. Petersburg.

She said, "These are for you. You can keep them. Thank you for today."

I can't remember ever being so frustrated. I wanted to kill her, but I also had liked her . . . the fury inside me would not go away.

The next day I took Miss Darling to the elevator, to return her to the third floor. I was still seething.

"Are you going to take me upstairs, young man?"

"Oh, yes," I said.

We got on the elevator.

"Remember, slowly and gently."

"Oh, yes, Miss Darling, I remember."

I threw that elevator into low gear and peeled that baby to the third floor like a rocket. ZOOM! When we reached the third floor I stopped it like we'd hit a wall and waited politely as Miss Darling, abashed, relieved herself on the elevator floor.

I knew as it happened that (a) I never should have done such a terrible thing to such a nice old lady, and (b) I would get fired. So that night I packed up and spent the night on a park bench, wondering how it could be that such sweet revenge had such a bitter taste.

9.

When I was 15 I was a gofer, and it was glorious. The job resulted from a chance meeting I had with William Saroyan, the great novelist, playwright, and screenwriter. I had been washing dishes at the Bright Angel's Lodge on the south rim of the Grand Canyon, and on a break I went outside to practice my banjo. Saroyan happened by, said he liked my style, gave me his card, and told me to look him up if I ever got to Los Angeles.

His name meant nothing to me at the time—I was only 15—but I did eventually get to L.A. I called him, and he invited me to meet him in his office at the MGM studios. It was through his kindness that I got the job as gofer.

I was one of a number of such lucky kids. We were asked to do many odd jobs, but we were also each assigned to a movie and told to study and pay attention to what the director was doing. If you were lucky, you might even get a one-liner.

We were surrounded by legends. Clark Gable, Spencer Tracy, Frank Morgan, John Garfield, Hedy Lamarr, Akim Tamiroff, Alan Jenkins, and dozens of other greats and near greats of Hollywood's heyday. On one of my first days there, at lunch in the cafeteria, I sat at a table with George Washington and Abraham Lincoln—actors working on a documentary about presidents. It took the better part of a year for me to get even a little used to such things.

Everything that happened out there seemed to be

magical, bigger than life. I remember when Clark Gable needed a tie clasp. No one had one, so he took a great big safety pin to hold his tie together. A few weeks later people were showing up wearing gold safety pins. They called them "Clark Gable Tie Clasps."

And pretty girls? When I first got there I said to myself, there goes the prettiest girl I've ever seen . . . no, she is . . . no, that one is.

One day I was told to go to the Irving Thalberg building and see the producer of *Tortilla Flats*. I was very excited. Why would the producer want to see me? I found out later a talent scout named Billy Grady had suggested me for a one-liner in the movie. The line was:

"Señor, your house is on fire!"

The Thalberg building was fascinating. Various producers had offices at the ends of a long hallway, with writers working in offices in between.

Those writers' offices may well have been the most interesting offices of all time. One of the perks that came with being a top writer at MGM was that you could have your office decorated any way you wanted. If you thought you could write better in an Old English–type cottage, that's what your office would become. I was told that Ben Hecht, a former newspaperman who wrote some of the all-time great movie scripts, had his office done up much like the city room of a metropolitan newspaper.

Well, I walked into the producer's office. His secretary became the latest most beautiful woman I had ever seen. I gave her my name, and she told me to have a seat. I sank about six feet deep in a soft leather chair and waited.

A moment later the door opened, and in walked Spencer Tracy.

I was dumbstruck. Here, in the same room with me,

was one of the world's great heroes. He was more than a star—a legend. He sat and waited, too. He nodded and smiled at me. Me!

The secretary then opened the door to the producer's office and said to me, "Come on in." I unsank myself from the chair and walked to the door, still staring in awe at Tracy.

Rumor had it that the studio purchased the rights to *Tortilla Flats* from John Steinbeck with the proviso that Tracy would have the lead, which he did.

So I walked into the room, and the producer glanced at me and said, "You'll do."

I turned around and came back out.

"Did you get the part?" Tracy asked me.

"Yes," I blurted out. Remember, we're talking about one line here: "Señor, your house is on fire." Yet this great actor, who was going to have the lead in the movie, wanted to know if I, Linn Sheldon, had got the job.

Then he said: "I hope I'm as lucky as you."

For a brief moment, I allowed myself to believe that Spencer Tracy really wanted to be as lucky as me. But it only lasted a moment—even at 15, I knew better—but what a great moment in my life that was!

Then, the first day on the set, he came over to me, shook my hand, and said: "We made it."

* * *

My part was left on the cutting room floor.

* * *

Girlwise, an MGM employee's badge was worth its weight in gold.

"You work at MGM? Gee . . . "

"Yes. I'm a producer there."

Now, I never said that. I was still in my late teens and looked younger than that, and I knew no one would believe I was a producer.

But they believed almost anything my friend Troy Vance would say. He was a reader in the reading department at the studio, and we double-dated a number of times. He was handsome and had a commanding way about him.

He also always seemed to have a new car.

When I asked him about that he explained he had a friend who owned a car dealership, and he let him take out the new cars to show them off. That was fine with me, and even finer with our dates.

During a short vacation I took I went on a fishing trip, and on the trip I met a very nice man named Martin. We fished together, and he told me he was some sort of judge. Judge Martin. I even had dinner with him and his wife.

When I got back to MGM I saw my friend Troy, and we made plans to double-date the following night. Again, we had a brand new car. The date went well, and we dropped the girls off in Beverly Hills, then headed back to our rooms in Culver City.

We were coming down one of the Beverly Hills streets when I heard a lot of sirens, and Troy slammed on the accelerator. We were doing 50, 60, 70 . . . in Beverly Hills, yet.

"Hey, Troy," I said, "take it easy." He looked scared to death. "We'll pay the ticket . . . just stop the car!" I yelled.

We came to a big, busy intersection, and he had no

choice but to stop. The police surrounded the car and hauled me out of the passenger seat, handcuffed me, and shoved me in the back seat of a patrol car. They put Troy in another car.

I'm going: "What is this? What's this all about?"

They said be quiet—you'll find out.

They took me to the Beverly Hills Police Department and put me in a room by myself. I remember the walls were pink. Maybe they were getting it ready for Eva Gabor.

I was petrified. What am I doing here? I wasn't even driving! I started to sing, just to calm myself down. A sergeant stuck his head in the door and told me to shut up. Obviously a man with no appreciation of the arts.

A while later the same sergeant opened the door and said, "This way."

He took me to the desk sergeant. In front of him is a piece of cardboard, and on it is everything I had in my pockets when they hauled me in.

As it turned out, Troy and another skinny guy who looked like me had robbed a bank of $25,000 the day before.

Troy would not tell the cops that I was not the accomplice, because whoever the real accomplice was still had the dough. So they figured it must be me.

Then they checked my alibi.

Where was I when the bank was robbed?

Fishing with Judge Martin.

* * *

When I was 17 I was an extra in a film called *The Painted Desert*.

It was one of those old, very low-budget "B" westerns, but I loved being involved because it brought together my two dreams of being an actor and a cowboy.

At the climax of the movie, the wagons were to go into a circle, and I would be a brave young man with a rifle trying to save my sister and my Ma. My Pa, I reckoned, was in a saloon somewhere back in Kansas.

On the day of the big shoot—I called it the day of the director's big mistake—the wagons were in a circle and Indians were racing around and everyone was shooting at everyone else. Lots of dust. Lots of noise.

Suddenly the director said: "Stop!" He was mad as hell.

"Now listen," he shouted through his megaphone. "Everyone is shooting, all right, but nobody is dying! What's going on?"

One of the Indians raised his hand and pointed out that the ground was full of jagged rocks, and no one was about to fall off a horse under those conditions.

We were all getting about four or five dollars a day for 10- or 12-hour days, just to be extras in a film. So the director said he'd pay another five bucks to anyone who would fall off his horse. He didn't designate anyone in particular.

We all took our positions.

"Roll 'em," said the director. Then "Action!"

Up over the rise came the Indians, whooping and hollering.

One guy fired his pistol. A single shot.

And every last Indian bit the dust.

* * *

When you start out in the entertainment field you set your sights very high—becoming a movie idol, playing the world's premier night clubs for the top dollar, critics comparing your Hamlet with John Barrymore's.

But along the way you do a lot of little things: be a clown at a restaurant; emcee a show in a rundown club, take a bit part in a live (this was pre-TV) radio show. You take these gigs because (a) you are broke; (b) you are lonely; (c) you are hungry. Five or six bucks? Let's do it! Get 15 bucks to emcee that hour-long show? Well, I guess I can. After all, I do have a week before my agent gets the word from the movie producer. (You know and they know there's no movie in your immediate future, but there is such a thing as preserving one's dignity, you know.)

It was one of those artistic side roads that, when I was in California, brought me to the theater . . . church? . . . tabernacle? . . . call it what you will, of the legendary evangelist, Aimee Semple McPherson.

Aimee was one of the most charismatic of all modern-day evangelists. The mind boggles at what she might have accomplished if television was around back then.

Her tabernacle was in Los Angeles, and, physically, it was more theater than church.

Her entrance was spectacular. A platform at the front of the stage could move up and down. The lights in the place dimmed, the orchestra played softly, and, on cue, soft lights mystically revealed Sister Aimee, her white silk gown draped halfway to the floor from arms raised to heaven, as she rose from the depths. The music grew to a crescendo, the lights got brighter and brighter, and the audience watched in stunned silence. They wanted to applaud, but could not. They just thanked God that she was there, and they were with her.

It was, to put is mildly, great drama.

What was my part in all of this?

I was at stage left, in the dark, and there was another young man, also in the dark, at stage right. The year was 1939, and people had begun worrying about the war in Europe and what would happen if we got mixed up in it. Aimee was tuned in to that, all right, and she told the congregation that if they lived as the Bible told them, they need not fear anything. God was on your side, she said. But if you sinned (as she did later in life) you would live in fear.

To illustrate and emphasize the fear, the lights would come up, and there I was, with my banjo, quivering in terror as I softly sang, of all things, the "Beer Barrel Polka." I shook in fear, waiting for the bombs to fall. I was all alone. God was with someone else.

On the other side of the stage was a strong young man with bright face and clear eyes, unafraid of anything life might have in store for him.

He was singing "Nearer My God to Thee."

In a way it was the story of my life and his. In spite of some later success, I was to drown my fear of life in booze.

The young man on the other side went on to great fame and fortune, and was a role model for strength and courage.

Anthony Quinn.

10.

Let me tell you about Hedy Lamarr and me.
If you are young, you might not know who Hedy Lamarr was, but if you are middle-aged or older, you certainly do. She was one of those legendary film beauties of the 1930s and '40s. Now, it may sound all too casual to say that I hung around with such beauties, but in fact I did spend the best two years of my teens at MGM doing wonderful but peripheral stuff, and if you were on the MGM lot you were always surrounded by some of the most beautiful women in the world.

For about three weeks I worked on the same set as Hedy Lamarr. The movie was *Tortilla Flats*, and its cast also included Spencer Tracy, John Garfield, Akim Tamiroff, and others. I was given the job of jogging with Akim Tamiroff to make sure he was convincingly out of breath for a certain scene.

On the day before Christmas, shooting ended early, and there was a party. Hedy Lamarr handed out little presents to everyone, and kissed each of us. It was the first time in my life I had seen professionally wrapped gifts. When it came my turn she gave me a box—some ties, as I recall—but didn't kiss me.

A little later I went back to her and said, "Miss Lamarr, how can I tell my grandchildren that you kissed everyone but me?

"Oh, Linn," she cooed, somehow saying it with a German accent, "come here."

I puckered up, and she kissed me. Right on the forehead.

Two years later, World War II was in full swing, and I found myself a sergeant in the army, stationed in Indiana. One night I was drinking beer with a bunch of GIs at a bar. We started talking about the movies, and I let it be known that I had worked at MGM. Somebody asked if I had ever met any of the pretty stars, and I told them I did. Certainly.

In my best, man-of-the-world manner I asked if any of them had heard of Hedy Lamarr. Of course they all had, and I had their immediate, rapt attention. I told them that she was even more beautiful in person. When they asked how well I knew her, I told them I wasn't free to answer that. That way, it was up to their imaginations. Soon someone asked if I planned on seeing her after the war. I told them sure, that we had talked about it.

"You talked about it? You're not engaged, or anything?"

Again, I told them I was not free to discuss that.

During this loud and beery conversation I had paid no attention to the group of civilians at a nearby table. One of them, it turned out, was a reporter for the *Indianapolis Times*. The next day the *Times* reported that Hedy Lamarr was engaged to a sergeant in the 83rd Division.

I was horrified.

Not as horrified as MGM. I got a steaming call from somebody important there, warning me against any such idiotic talk in the future.

I was 21 back then. I wonder if she still waits for me.

Show Business
in Cleveland

I am now 22 years old and fresh out of the army. Since I am discharged near my home, I enroll as a student at the Cleveland Play House, one of the world's premier repertoire/training theaters.

In my first role I play the part of a smoking dinosaur, although it wasn't written that way, and in another play the whole cast comes down with diarrhea, but the show goes on—strangely.

I also hone my stand-up comedy routines at local nightclubs, and before long I am drawn into the new medium that will change the world's history and culture—television.

It is so new, in fact, that there are only about a thousand sets in all of northeastern Ohio, each showing black-and-white images that tend to go in and out of focus. Thus the few of us who enter the field are pioneers of the medium in the truest sense, and if the images the public sees are in black and white, life for us is more colorful than ever.

11.

When I got out of the army in the mid-'40s, I knew I wanted to stay in show business, and the GI Bill gave me the chance I needed to get some legitimate theater training.

I knew that natural talent by itself was not enough to succeed. For that, I would have to know and understand the craft of theater, and that meant a lot of hard work.

I thought first about joining the Pasadena Playhouse, which would keep me physically close to Hollywood, but I had also heard a lot about the Cleveland Play House and its founders, Frederick McConnell and K. Elmo Lowe. It was also close to my hometown of Norwalk, and within blocks of where I was given my discharge.

Back then the Play House was a superb repertoire theater and a legendary spawning ground for actors, actresses, directors, and other theater professionals.

You paid for the privilege of studying there.

How good was it? If its graduates are any measure (and they certainly are) it was great. They included Paul Newman, Tom Hanks, Ray Walston, Dom De Luise, Jack Weston, and many more. Another was Margaret Hamilton. She was one of the sweetest women I've ever met, and she played one of the meanest females in film history, the Wicked Witch of the West in The *Wizard of Oz*.

I met with Mr. McConnell and asked if I could enroll at the Play House and have it paid for through the GI Bill. He said he didn't know—no one had ever tried it before. But it worked out fine, and I became the first person, though hardly the last, to study at the Cleveland Play House that way.

I began as a stagehand, building sets, getting props, pulling the curtain, listening to direction, taking tickets: in short, learning every aspect of the craft from the ground up, and learning it well.

My first role came about because I was the skinniest guy around. Thornton Wilder's Pulitzer Prize–winning play, *The Skin of Our Teeth*, was a kind of history of the world and its thought. In it, he had written a part for a dinosaur.

The Play House managed to get the original dinosaur costume from the New York show. It had a huge papier-mâché head with jaws opened wide, showing a mouthful of big, ugly teeth. The actor inside could look out through the jaws and see what was going on. Since I was the only one who could fit in the costume, I got the part.

So much for natural talent.

In one scene the male lead, Clerry Cavanaugh, was smoking a cigarette. When he threw it away, the dinosaur was supposed to go over and step on it. One night he flicked the cigarette, but missed the floor. Instead, the lit cigarette went into the open jaws and settled about six inches from my nose.

At first, all I could think to do was spit at the cigarette.

That didn't work, so I ad-libbed, "I want to go out and chase a car . . . " and off I went, stage left.

And now you know, class, why dinosaurs are extinct. It wasn't a meteor.

* * *

There are times when the phrase "the show must go on" gives rise to a kind of wondrous absurdity.

As Rod Serling used to say, case in point . . .

The Cleveland Play House was doing a production of Paul Osborne's adaptation of John Hersey's novel, *A Bell for Adano*. It is a great play about an American officer, Major Victor Joppolo, and a group of GIs in Italy in World War II who win the hearts of the people in the town of Adano by getting the bell for their tower back from the Germans, who had stolen it.

The part of Major Joppolo was played by Ed Binns, who went on to do some fine work in films . . . as General Bedel Smith in Patton, one of the jurors in *Twelve Angry Men*, and in other roles.

After one of the evening performances there was a party, with cheese and Italian red wine generously donated by the father of one of the cast. Generous is putting it mildly. There was enough Chianti to keep the whole town of Adano loaded for a week.

Everybody knew they should get home early, since there was a matinee the next day.

What they didn't know was that the wine, the cheese, or both, were bad. Every person in the cast showed up that afternoon with a terrible case of diarrhea. Toilets were flushing everywhere. Teeth clenched and walking funny, they all assured the director there was no way they could go on.

The director, himself sick, said, "Who cares! We've GOT to do it . . . there are PEOPLE out there," and headed for the nearest biffy.

So we did the show, but to this day I don't know how we got through it. I do remember that it took about an hour longer than normal, because people would kind of dissolve off stage and run to the johns, and the play would just have to slow down until they got back.

I also remember when Jack Weston, one of the more distinguished Play House graduates, had an attack he said, "Excuse me . . . I have to go put a nickel in the parking meter." Of course, there were no parking meters in *Bell For Adano* but the rest of the cast picked up on that, and throughout the play one actor after another left the stage to "put a nickel in that parking meter." If you waited about six or seven beats—BOOM . . . you'd hear a toilet flush.

There's one scene where one of the players is supposed to pull a gun on Major Joppolo, and the two get into a serious wrestling match. As one of the villagers, I was waiting to make an entrance and watching what was happening on stage—more specifically, what was not happening.

The guy never pulled the gun.

He just stood there, with a kind of glazed look on his face, struggling to control his inner self, so to speak.

When the other actor failed to pull out the gun, Ed Binns, assuming the guy had forgotten his line, ad-libbed, "I suppose you're going to pull out your gun now."

And the guy replied, "Not today, I'm not."

* * *

I've known a lot of twins in my time, but none to compare with the Anderson Brothers.

Walter and Bill Anderson were as identical as could be, and handsomer than any men had a right to be. In their late thirties, they had blue eyes, salt-and-pepper hair, great smiles, identical voices, and enormous charm. And, like moths to a flame, a great many women were attracted to them.

In the mid-1940s, Bill and Walt and I were on a national tour with a show called *Rosalie*. I played the part of Bill Delroy in the play, and they were the stage managers. Walt was the head guy and Bill was second in charge, although no one was ever quite sure which Anderson was which. Nor did anyone care much, for the twins were such likable and competent men.

Many nights on the road the three of us would share hotel quarters, not only because together we could get a suite, which was nicer than an individual room, but also because we thoroughly enjoyed each other's company.

One night—in St. Paul, Minnesota—Bill and I were sitting in our suite when Walt phoned to say he was bringing a lady up.

"Fine . . . okay . . . gotcha," said Bill.

He told me to climb into my bed in the corner of the room and pretend to be asleep. Then he took off all his clothes and opened a window—not much, about a foot— then turned off all the lights. You could scarcely see in the darkness of that room. Then he went into the bathroom, got in the shower, and pulled the curtain across.

I remember thinking the twins had done this particular kind of stage managing more than once. Every move was crisp, efficient, and productive.

Enter Walt, as the script might say, with two pounds of charm, a beguiling smile, and one of the most beautiful women I have ever seen. Within minutes they were making love in the other bed in the room. When they were finished Walt said: "Don't leave, my darling. I'll be right back."

He goes into the bathroom, pulls the shower curtain back, and runs the water. His brother gets out of the shower, Walter gets in. The water stops, Bill gets into bed with the woman and says, "I missed you, my darling."

"Ah," purred the lady moments later. "You're the best."

12.

My three former wives, like my present one, had three things in common: great beauty, uncommon patience, and, I like to think, great taste in men. Well, at least they had the first two in common.

As I look back, each wife seems to have come into my life at a distinct stage in my development as a husband, an adult, and an actor and entertainer.

Ruth was there at the beginning. Beautiful (she had been a beauty queen at Ohio State University), smart, and competent, she meshed right into my budding career. When I was at the Cleveland Play House she got a job in its front office. When I was at Cain Park she got office work there.

We lived in a rented room in a house in the eastern Cleveland suburb of Cleveland Heights, not far from the Play House or Cain Park. To say that we were poor is understating the case. But Ruth was as tough and persistent as she was beautiful, and she managed somehow to cope with our room-and-a-hot-plate existence.

If you've seen the movie *True Grit* you have a good measure for Ruth.

Even when she became pregnant with Linda, our oldest daughter, and had to quit working, her spirits and toughness never flagged.

Although she never mentioned it to me, she burned her hand on the hot plate, a day or two before she went into labor. Those pains started on a very dark and very stormy night, with great slashes of lightning and crashing peals of thunder. Without a car, I suddenly panicked. I called the Yellow Cab Company and pleaded with the dispatcher to send a cab as soon as possible—that the baby was on the way.

Within minutes a cab pulled up, and we got in. The driver was as nervous as I was, as we sped toward St. Luke's Hospital. Just before we got there, Ruth said the pains were increasing, and in an effort to comfort her I held her hand tightly.

The burned hand.

She let out a yelp of pain, and the driver twisted his head around.

"Is it coming?" he shouted. "Is it coming?"—and very nearly whacked into a big elm tree. I'm sure he was as relieved as I was when we made it to the hospital in time.

* * *

Things got increasingly busy for me. In addition to shows at the Play House and Cain Park, I was in a road company doing *Rosalie*. I was also beginning to get some regular late-night work as a stand-up comic at the Alpine Village.

The shift in my life was on, although I didn't know at the time how great that shift would be. Until then, most of my efforts were devoted to acting, especially in musicals. While life in the theater was loose enough, and many of its practitioners, including me, kept nicely lubricated with wine and liquor, it still commanded a certain respect. People actually paid money to come see you (or the play) onstage.

Nightclub entertaining was entirely different. Here, you stood in front of a bunch of people whose goal that evening was to get drunk or pick up a companion for the night, and who for the most part shouldn't be permitted to drive home. The bartender was the comic's best friend.

At least, this comic's.

The more I worked the nightclub circuit, the more I drank, and the more I worked and drank, the less of a husband and father and provider I became.

We still had no car and, it seemed, even less money. I would make the 100-mile round trip from Norwalk to Cleveland and back by Greyhound bus. In fact, to save money I kept a toothbrush and toothpaste in one jacket pocket and a razor in the other and spent a number of nights sleeping on a bench in the Greyhound terminal at East 9th Street and Superior Avenue.

One night, shortly before Christmas, I had a better than usual paycheck from the Alpine Village. I bought a small present for Ruth, and a smaller one for Linda. I also bought something I had needed badly—a warm overcoat.

I finished my work at the Alpine Village and walked down to the bus terminal, enjoying the warmth of that coat every step of the way. I got on the 1:00 A.M. bus, said hi to Brownie, the regular driver on that run, folded up the coat, put it in the storage rack over the seats, and sat down next to an old man who looked as tired and poor as I felt.

I slept soundly during the two-hour trip, until Brownie stopped the bus at the corner of street where we lived.

Still groggy, I got up and walked toward the front of

the bus. The old man, bless his heart, said, "Hey—you forgot this," and threw my coat to me.

I thanked him, went out the door, and the bus took off.

It was very cold, and as I put my arm in one sleeve, it almost fell apart. It was the old man's coat. He not only had my new coat, but if he had a wife and baby daughter, a couple of nice little gifts for them.

Ho, ho, ho.

* * *

It's not hard to figure out why Ruth and I separated. I was home less and less, drinking more and more, and becoming ever more adept at telling myself that my career deserved more attention than she or Linda did.

She did give me as great a gift as anyone could have given me.

Linda.

Today Linda is one of the prime movers in the women's fashion industry. Having held top positions with Giorgio Armani and Calvin Klein, she now is executive vice president of sales and merchandising for the fashion house of Valentino.

I'll tell you about my other wives and children a little later on.

13.

Let's take a long look at Cleveland as I knew it when I began my career in earnest.

During World War II and into the early '50s, Cleveland probably had more nightclubs than any other city in the country outside of New York and Chicago.

The city also became a launching pad for a number of successful orchestras—Guy Lombardo and Sammy Kaye, to mention two. That's because at the time, when radio was still king, Cleveland had a 50,000-watt radio station, WTAM, and the networks asked all 50,000-watters to program two to three hours of network feed from their call letters. Thus quality orchestras would come to Cleveland just to get on the radio in order to sell themselves to other cities throughout the country.

There were nightclubs up and down Euclid Avenue and on side streets from downtown to East 107th Street. I had some favorites: the Cabin Club, which had Redd Foxx as emcee and great bands and a lot of dancing; Lindsey's Sky Bar, and Chin's Chinese, both of which featured such legendary jazz pianists as Art Tatum and Fats Waller, and boogie-woogie masters Meade Lux Lewis and Albert Ammons. Moe's Main Street offered the song stylings of Tony Benedetto, whom you know as Tony Bennett, and later Johnnie Raye, who wept his way through "The Little White Cloud That Cried." Dean Martin was singing at the Hollenden Hotel.

Borselino's Restaurant also booked nightclub acts,

and I worked there with a trio called "The Three Sons" and a short, baby-faced singing star named Bobby Breen. One night he and I went over to the Statler Hotel at East 12th and Euclid. There, a singer named Karl Brisson was holding forth with George Duffy's orchestra. Very tall, very handsome, and suaver than suave in top hat and tails, he would serenade the ladies at the tables and make them wish they had never married.

On the way back Breen said he thought he could do something like that, and the next night, sure enough, he showed up in top hat, white tie, and tails, and began crooning to a beautiful young woman in a table up front.

She looked at him, smiled maternally, and said: "Why don't you go home and get your father?"

I was able to get work in several other clubs as a stand-up comic and emcee, but the one that helped me most—and that I enjoyed the most—was the Alpine Village, a creation of a German-born gentleman named Herman Pirchner and his two brothers.

As you entered the club you would pass (or perch at) a nice little bar that attracted businessmen in search of a buffer between work and home. Then there was a stairway leading to the second floor and a charming room with soft lights, good food, a dance floor, and live music—a room for lovers.

But the big attraction was beyond: a theater-restaurant that seated between three and four hundred people. It had a big stage and a band shell for the house band, a fine 14-piece orchestra led by a trumpet player named Frankie Stracek. There was a line of showgirls who could sing and dance with the best anywhere, called "The Lindsey Ladies."

The orchestra, the showgirls, a man named Bill Boehm (who later founded the Singing Angels), and I comprised a company that performed abbreviated versions of Broadway shows, like *Brigadoon* and *Finian's Rainbow*, with an occasional Gilbert and Sullivan operetta thrown in. Each little production ran only 12 to 15 minutes, and we would do them twice on weeknights and three times on Saturday nights.

I also got to work with some of the great comedians of the day: among them a stuttering comic named Joe Frisco and the great circus clown, Emmett Kelly.

Joe Frisco stuttered badly but instead of concealing it made it an integral part of his schtick. He was the comedian's comedian—the one other performers talked about. While neither he nor any other comedian enjoyed the instant fame and amazing exposure that television can bring today (even to second- and third-rate performers), Joe Frisco was right at the top of his craft.

He was always broke, though, mostly because he could not stay away from the racetrack. When he came to Cleveland he would head for a small track between there and Akron called Ascot, and I would often go with him. We were in the clubhouse one day, and the horses were pounding down the stretch when the jockey fell off the horse Joe had bet on.

"Joe," I said. "Your jockey fell off the horse!"

"Wi . . . wi . . . wi . . . with my luck, he j . . . j . . . j . . . jumped."

Once Joe was in Chicago and in need of some fast cash. He managed to steal a very nice copy of DaVinci's *Last Supper*, which he took to a pawnshop. When the guy asked him how much he wanted for it, Joe said, "Twa . . . twa . . . twa . . . twenty dollars a plate."

He was thrown into jail one time, charged with setting his hotel bed on fire. The judge asked him if he did it.

"I'm innocent," said Joe.

"Why do you say that?" asked the judge.

"Because the ba . . . ba . . . ba . . . .ba . . . bed was on fire when I got in it."

He once owed Bing Crosby $10,000. When he saw Crosby in the clubhouse of a racetrack Crosby owned, Joe had just won a lot of money. Crosby looked at him as if to say, "Where's my ten grand?" and Joe said, "Hey, kid. Ain't you the singer?"

Crosby smiled and said yes, he was.

Frisco slid a twenty-dollar bill toward him and said, "Here, sing me a chorus of, 'Meh . . . Meh . . . Meh . . . Melancholy Baby.'"

One last Joe Frisco story.

He was at a benefit in New York City along with a long list of great vaudeville stars, with the great operatic tenor, Enrico Caruso, as the featured attraction.

Caruso was warming up, going up and down the scales, thrilling not only himself but all those within earshot. As other performers hovered around in awe of the great man, Friscoe walked up to him and said:

"Hey, Rico. Don't sing 'Da . . . Da . . . Da . . . Darktown Strutter's Ball.' That's mine," and walked away.

One of the men I most enjoyed working with was Emmett Kelly, perhaps the world's most famous circus clown, the creator of Willie, the Tramp and as great a mime as ever lived.

Few people remembered that Kelly had begun his career as a newspaper cartoonist, and that Willie was first born as one of his cartoon characters.

I was delighted when he asked me to do a little piece

with him in the opening of his act. The entire act was done without either of us saying a word. It opened with the spotlight following this poor, bedraggled tramp as he entered the room, confused, not knowing where he was, and obviously in search of someone who might ease his loneliness. It was all written in his face and his every move, and clear as day. Finding no one, he would wander up on the stage, where he discovered an immaculate table set with a white cloth, fine china and silverware, flowers, the works. To sit or not to sit, that was the question.

Such was his magic that the simple act of this poor, sad man dressed in tatters finally sitting down at that table was at once hilarious and moving.

I played the part of the waiter. I would hand him the menu, and then he'd look up. I would gesture: do you want a cocktail? He would shake his head—no—and make a big circle with his hands. No question about that—he wanted a whole bucket of beer. Then he would order an entire meal, and you knew just what each dish was—chicken, vegetables, potatoes, pie—everything, and I would leave.

Still in the spotlight he would look at the utensils, find fault with and polish each one. Finally, he would notice something on the horribly ragged coat he wore—a piece of lint. With an flick of his finger, the offending lint would be dispatched. I have never seen such elegant, convincing pantomime: he would take the audience from laughter to tears in seconds.

I would then bring out an easel and some charcoal, and he would do quick but brilliant caricatures of people in the audience—signed drawings that are worth a pretty penny today. Each time he would measure each subject with his thumb, as artists will. At the close of his act he would tear off the last sheet and show it to the audience. It was a portrait of his thumb.

He had a unique way of handling hecklers. When one started up, Kelly would take the easel right down in front of the guy and stare him right in the eyes, then start measuring his forehead, his nose, and his chin and start sketching.

When he was finished he turned the picture around for the audience, and there was the ugliest-looking jackass, mouth wide open, that you have ever seen. As the audience applauded he tore off the sheet and handed it to the guy, who likely never heckled anyone ever again.

There were dozens more top-of-their-trade comics, actors, jugglers, magicians, acrobats, and musicians that worked the Alpine Village, and I learned from all of them. It was like being at some marvelous school for performers, and a wonderful extension of the serious work I was still doing at the Cleveland Play House.

Then one evening someone, I don't remember who it was, told me that a television station was about to start up in Cleveland, and suggested I go down there and see if they could use someone of my talents.

The next day I headed down to the station on East 13th Street, just behind the venerable old Sterling-Lindner-Davis department store, to see what I could see.

And the rest, as they say, is history.

14.

Have you ever looked at the cover girl on a magazine and thought, "Boy, I'd give anything to know a woman like that!"?

If you're a male, you probably have.

Well I have, and I did.

Her name was Vivian, and she was about as beautiful as people of the feminine persuasion get to be. I fell in love with her before I ever saw her. Her picture was on the cover of a magazine—she was a Powers model—and she was, not to put too fine a point on it, stunning. The only thing more beautiful than her picture was Vivian herself. And if ever there was the antithesis to the dumb blonde, it was Vivian. She had gone to Oberlin College, working her way through for as long as she could afford to do so.

After my marriage to Ruth had been put asunder, I kept on bouncing from theater to nightclub to theater and, now, to a new medium: television.

Vivi and I met while I was doing stand-up comedy at the Alpine Village. As I say, I had seen her picture on the cover of a magazine, and when one night I saw her sitting with a man at a table I knew it was her, and I knew I had to meet her.

When I finished my bit I went to the maître d' at the reservation podium and found out the man's name. Then I phoned a friend and told him to call back and have the man paged, then tell him anything to keep him on the line for a minute or two.

It worked like a charm. I watched as the maître d' answered his phone, went to the table to tell Vivian's escort that he had a call, and led him off to a booth. Vivian was alone. I walked to the table, introduced myself to her, said something nice about her picture, and said I would like to call her, all in one breath.

To my astonishment and delight, she said she would like that, and gave me her phone number.

The man returned just as I left.

On a cloud.

* * *

We hit it off right away, and for a long time everything was uphill.

Vivian was a realist, and that made her a first-rate manager. She saw me for what I was, still very much a boy at heart who drank too much, and with little sense of purpose and not the slightest idea of how to move his career ahead.

So she began to manage me.

It was Vivian who introduced me to DeArv Barton of MCA, the nation's top booking agency, and it was Vivian who handled the business dealings with local television, nightclubs, and theaters and just about anything else connected with my career.

Not only that, she also appeared with me for a number of months on a morning-coffee-type talk show called *The Sheldons*.

At the same time I was doing a show called *Charades*, a weekly show called *Big Wheels*, and a daily piece called *The Linn Sheldon Show*. What's more, Barnaby was born and was becoming popular, and DeArv Barton was booking me in places as far away as Texas.

I was all over the place, and Vivian was at my side, making sure that my naiveté did not get the best of me—that I went forward and not backward.

The result was something I had always wanted, but had never known: a real home of my own. This one was in Parma Heights, with a gorgeous and loving wife, and not one, but two cars in the driveway.

As great as those gifts were—for they were all things created by her and handed to me—they paled in comparison with the two children she gave birth to, Abbigail and Perry. Like their stepsister, Linda, they are among the more beautiful people in this world.

Perhaps the stability that all that brought frightened me as much as it pleased me, for I kept on drinking and misbehaving or, when I was doing neither of those, trying to make it up to this beautiful creature.

Then the most terrible thing happened. Vivian was diagnosed with two inoperable brain tumors, and given a year to live.

There's not a lot to say about that, except the cancer attacked both her brain and her face.

All that beauty of mind and body, laid to waste. Two beautiful children devastated, a husband lost again.

Vivian died seven months later, on Valentine's Day.

* * *

Abbigail became a registered nurse, then an advanced clinical nurse, and is now helping patients get better and doctors get smarter at University Hospitals in Cleveland.

Perry is a producer of sports in Florida and the Caribbean for the Sunshine Television Network. After serving four years in the U.S. Air Force he took up parachuting as a sport, and became more than expert at it. He in fact made the *Guiness Book of World Records* by planning, organizing, and executing the largest mass jump ever—more than 130 parachutists, hand in hand in a globe formation, plummeting toward the ground.

Perry once talked me into putting on a parachute and going up in a light plane with him. "It will be fun, Dad," he said. But I knew better. When the time came for me to step out of that open door, I froze.

"What's wrong, Dad?" he shouted over the whistling wind.

"I'm not going to jump out of a plane," I said, "holding hands with one of the beneficiaries on my insurance policy."

And I didn't.

15.

When no one can tell you what to be, all you can be is yourself. That's how it was in February of 1948, when I went to work for Cleveland's first television station, WEWS.

The station had been operating for less than two months and was one of the first television stations in the country. On air with me were four others: Dorothy Fuldheim, Alice Weston, Paul Hodges, and Bob Dale.

As with all pioneering efforts, being the first meant there was no one around to tell us how to look, how to sit, what to do in front of the camera. Without instruction there is no choice but to summon up some courage, be yourself, and hope the people like you. In fact, if there were only one thing I could tell young people coming into the communications business today or in the future, it is that: be yourself.

One thing about that time still puzzles me. Within two months of our being on air, one of the local universities began offering a course in television communications. Where they learned the trade and how to teach it I'll never know.

Compared with today's standards, early television was caveman technology. At WEWS we had three huge cameras, all on wooden tripods. Each camera had three lenses on a turret. If, for example, we needed a close-up shot of Bob Dale, followed by a long shot, the director would have to take the picture with one camera while the lens was manually changed on the other. After you got the full-length shot you'd have to go back to the other camera.

We had boom microphones—mikes at the ends of long arms mounted on rollers. The mike would be positioned a little ahead of and above you, and the boom operator would have to turn it and follow you wherever you went. If you danced and sang at the same time, which I sometimes did, they had a tough time following.

One time we had a new boom operator, and I had as a guest a ventriloquist. Every time the dummy spoke, the guy turned the mike toward the dummy. That tells you how good the guest was and how new the technology was. The lights were called scoops. They looked like half-eggshells with 5,000-watt bulbs. With 20 or so scoops beating down on you the heat was terrific. On occasion, one of the guys would pull down a light to heat up his lunch.

Today, almost everything is on tape, but as long as we were on the air back then there was a man in the announcer's booth for station breaks and other pronouncements. Cort Stanton manned our booth.

If we used recorded sound, music or voice, it was on 78 rpm records at first, then 45's, and finally tape.

Today's control board looks like something out of *Star Wars*. In 1948 it looked more like it had been *in* a war. The producers had little more to deal with than on-off switches for the three cameras and a few other buttons that they understood but I never tried to figure out.

The studio was half the size of a basketball court. The offices, except for those of the president, general manager, and sales manager, were on the second floor. Everyone else was in one room, which was bigger than the studio, and shared the desks. That had its advantages: if you wanted to talk to someone in sales, all you had to do was holler across the room.

My first job was to go on the air at the very beginning of each broadcast day—normally about four in the afternoon—and tell the viewers what they would see that day. Most days we began with a kinescope of singer Johnny Desmond and his band. Kinescope was a big thing then. It was a film made by putting a camera next to a television set and filming what was on its screen. Most kinescopes were made in New York or California and shipped to stations around the country. By today's standards their quality was terrible, but because the medium was so new their impact was sensational.

If it wasn't Johnny Desmond it would be Fred Waring and his Pennsylvanians, or Arthur Godfrey, followed by movies, cartoons and the efforts of our on-air personalities. Others like *The Cisco Kid* and *Hopalong Cassidy*, all in black and white, of course, were wildly popular: again testifying more to the compelling newness of the medium than to the quality of the shows.

There were fewer than a thousand TV sets in the entire Northeast Ohio area when 1948 rolled around, and many of those were in saloons and department stores. It was not unusual to see a crowd peering into a store window, all mesmerized by discernible if somewhat ghostly black-and-white images on small screens.

The first home sets were made by Hallicrafters, Du-Mont, and a company started by a character named Madman Muntz. DuMont had set up the first network, beating ABC, CBS, and NBC to the punch.

Local programming included Dorothy Fuldheim, who did the news and commentary and who was to keep on doing it into the 1980s. Alice Weston did a cooking show. Bob Dale did a show called *Dinner Platter*, and Paul Hodges did interviews and later on a show called *Dress and Guess*, in which he would dress up in a costume and the viewer was supposed to guess who he was.

Now is that a kinder, gentler time, or what?

When I announced what was coming up each day, I always did a little comedy schtick, played the banjo, sang a song, or lip-synched a record. Lip-synching meant a 78 rpm record would be played in the control room, then piped out over the public address system so it could be heard in the studio. I would silently mouth the words, as if I were singing the song.

Lip-synching was nothing new. It had been done in the movies all the time so that the Nelson Eddys and Jeanette MacDonalds of the world could look as if they were reaching difficult notes without contorting their classic features.

One day a man named Fred Schall, who was with the ad agency that represented the Rogers Jewelry chain in the region, asked me if I could lip-synch twice a week, on Tuesdays and Thursdays, for 15 minutes. Of course I could, and thus what became known as The Linn Sheldon Show became the first show in Ohio to be fully sponsored by a single advertiser.

In the fall of 1948 the Cleveland Indians won the American League baseball championship. When it was announced that the World Series would be televised live, the sales of home TV sets went through the roof.

We were off and running!

* * *

Everybody came to work early, even the secretaries, the engineers—everybody.

That's how exciting, how much fun it was in the early days. We were entertaining an ever-growing public, and it was just great.

The only arguments we had were about what we were going to do on air, but they were quickly and easily settled. No animosity. No jealousy. I think a key reason was that we were in such a state of wonderment at it all.

If you weren't around at that time, it's probably not possible to fully understand the hypnotic nature of this new medium. For example, if you turned your set on before the regular programs went on the air you would see a test pattern—a series of lines, squares, and circles to help you adjust your set for a better picture. The test pattern, in black and white, had no motion at all; it just kind of sat there. But in those early days it was not unusual to go into a bar that had a TV and find everyone at the bar staring at that test pattern.

I remember talking with Dorothy Fuldheim about it.

"Some day," she said, "we'll be coming into people's homes so often they'll begin to think they know us and we know them."

And that came true. More than once I'd be walking down the street when someone would come up to me and say something like: "Hey, Linn, Fred and his wife moved to Pittsburgh and Josephine had a baby . . . " and I didn't know this person, Fred, Josephine, or their baby. But we came into their homes so often they really felt we knew them as well as they knew us.

They also would write in just to say hello or "saw you on the air . . . "—to anyone and, on occasion, anything they saw on the tube. One day we wondered what would happen if we put a still picture of someone on the set over and over again. We put up a photograph of President Franklin Roosevelt, and within a few days letters started coming in to him, care of the station: "Hello, President Roosevelt. We saw you on the show . . . ." One day we put up Joseph Stalin's photo, and, sure enough, old Uncle Joe got two fan letters that week.

I know that doesn't sound possible, but like the man says, you hadda be there to believe it.

* * *

Because of the tremendous heat generated by the studio lights, we would often keep a door to the outside open. There was no air conditioning. It would get so hot our makeup would melt and run down our faces.

With the door open, anyone walking past the building could, if they had a mind to, come in. Right near the door was a wall that divided two sets—a cooking show on one side and an interview set on the other. There was a door in the middle of this set.

I was out there one day when someone rapped on that door. I opened it, and there stood some guy I had never seen before. He asked me if there was a men's room, because he had to go real bad. I told him it was right down the hall. In a few minutes he came back to thank me, then he looked around, saw the camera with its little red light on, and said, "My God! Am I on television?" and literally ran away.

* * *

One day a fireman from outside the city came through town promoting the advantages of a new type of fire extinguisher.

He was a big, rugged-looking man of about 240 pounds. He had with him a shiny new fire extinguisher and about 25 pieces of butcher's paper.

The director asked if he would like to have someone on the set with him during the 10-minute segment, but the fireman assured him he had made the pitch many times on radio and could do it himself, thank you very much. The set was very simple, just a chair and a desk with a globe on it, a metal wastebasket next to it, an American flag behind it and a big, panoramic view of Yellowstone Park in the background.

Before the show he asked to use a telephone, and called his wife to tell her to be sure to watch.

The chair he would sit in was surrounded by monitors, so you could see yourself from any given angle. If you weren't used to this, it could be very disconcerting.

Time for the show. Number one camera dollied in, and the man saw himself on the monitor, coming toward him no less, and he started to shrink into that chair. The closer it came, the more he shrank.

The floor director cued him to speak.

The fireman cleared his throat.

"Harrumph!" he choked, but he couldn't get a real word out of his mouth.

In a panic he grabbed one of the pieces of butcher paper, set fire to it, threw it into the metal wastebasket, let it blaze up, then doused it with the new fire extinguisher.

Nine minutes to go.

Still unable to speak, he kept harrumphing and setting papers on fire and putting them out with the extinguisher. Four minutes to go, and he ran out of paper. He opened the desk drawer and pulled out whatever was in there, set fire to it, and put it out. When there were but two minutes left to go, he pulled out his handkerchief, set fire to it, and put it out.

I told the director I'd better get over there before the guy set fire to Yellowstone National Park and the American flag.

I went out and said, "What a marvelous fire extinguisher that is, sir."

The fireman got up and walked straight out of the building, fast.

I wondered what happened if he got home and his wife opened the door and said, "I saw you . . . ."

He probably let her have it with the fire extinguisher.

* * *

One of the most talented people I have ever known was a man named Gene Carroll.

Long before television came on the scene—and for some years afterward—Gene and his partner, Glenn Rowell, were on local and network radio with a show called *Gene and Glenn*. Gene is probably best remembered for two of the characters he created and also played on the show, Jake and Lena.

He was also heavily involved in the earliest days of television, and was a tremendous help later on as I developed Barnaby.

At the time I was, in effect, the opening act for each day's broadcasting, telling the audience what was coming up, interviewing people, and doing songs, comedy bits, and anything else I could think of.

When I first met Gene, I asked him if he would come on my show that day, and he said he would.

A little later his wife came up to me and said, "Be careful of that guy. He's a sweetheart, but sometimes he'll throw you a curve, just for the fun of it."

We got together to talk about the show, and Gene asked me what I'd like to do. I told him I'd love to sing a song that he and Glenn sang on their radio show, with Glenn singing melody and Gene doing the harmony.

"Fine," he said. "Which one should we do?"

"How about 'When They Cut Down That Old Pine Tree'?"

He said okay, but we'd better rehearse it. We sat down at the piano. He played, and we worked out the harmonies for about a half hour, just before the show.

We went on the air, live of course. I did a number and then introduced Gene.

"Well, what should we do tonight?" he asked.

"How about singing one of those great old songs you and Glenn used to sing on the radio?"

He said okay, and we sat down at the piano.

"Which one do you want to sing?" asked Gene.

"When They Cut Down That Old Pine Tree," said I.

"Gee," he said. "I don't remember that one. We never sang a song like that. Now here's one we did do . . . " and he started playing something I'd never heard before.

I really got befuddled. "C'mon, Gene," I pleaded, "we rehearsed that other one for some time . . . "

Then he said, "Sure, I'm just joking," and moved right into "When They Cut Down That Old Pine Tree."

As much as anything else, that brought home one of

the most valuable lessons any entertainer can learn: never drop your guard.

Later on that night we and our wives went out to dinner. For dessert I ordered pumpkin pie. Before I could stick my fork into the pie I was called to the phone. Having had Lesson Number 1 that very day on Gene's shenanigans, I wrote a quick note on the tablecloth, next to the pie. It said: "Don't eat this. I spit on it."

When I returned Gene had written, "So did I."

16.

Back in the '50s I had a television show in Cleveland called Big Wheels. The show was originally done in Cincinnati by a man named Red Thornburg. We negotiated with him to produce it in northern Ohio. I thought then and I still think today it was one of the best shows for children ever put on the air. Given the ocean of idiocies brought before children today, someone would do very well to bring this concept back.

The idea was that children would write and tell us what they'd like to be when they grow up, and why. The letters poured in from kids who dreamed of being pilots, nurses, athletes, artists, policemen, doctors—you name it.

The writer of the best letter would get to spend a day being just what he or she wanted to be.

The first winner, I recall, wanted to be a pilot. We called United Airlines, and they loved the idea. They got a uniform for the youngster, a boy of six or seven, let him sit in the pilot's seat (while the plane was on the ground, of course), gave him a tour of the control tower, and really showed him what a pilot's life was all about.

One of the beauties of the show was the opportunity it gave the companies that participated to show their products and people at their very best. Coming off as an organization that loves kids has to be a very powerful public relations coup. Hardly had the first show ended before American Airlines called to let us know they would be delighted to help if some young girl wrote in wanting to be a stewardess; a gourmet restaurant said they would be happy to accommodate a youngster who wanted to be a chef; a bank offered a $50 deposit and a savings deposit box to a kid who wanted to be a banker; one girl sat in on a rehearsal with the Cleveland Orchestra, and so on.

Years later I learned that some of the children who won in fact went on to become what they had aspired to be.

Louis Seltzer, the powerful editor of the old *Cleveland Press*, called me and said he could help a youngster who wanted to be a movie star. We talked to the head of the Coca-Cola bottling company, who sponsored our show, and he said he would go all out—fly us out to California in his private plane, the works.

So we went on the air and asked, "Would you like to be a movie star? Tell us why in 25 words or less."

That brought in a mountain of mail—more than 30,000 responses. It seems that about 75 percent of them, obviously written with the aid of their parents, said they wanted to be a movie star so they could make a lot of money and come back and help the poor.

Our heartstrings were not tugged.

Instead we were charmed by a little girl who wrote: "I am not talented. I can't sing or dance or anything like that. I just would like to go because I know it will be the only time in my life I'll get to be a movie star."

Once the girl was selected, Mr. Seltzer called Bob Hope, who was filming at Paramount Studios. Hope invited the winner, her family, me, and our crew to come to California. He would see to it that the girl would have a small walk-on part in the movie he was shooting, *Son of Paleface*.

Mr. Hope also called me and asked if we would like

to come to his home for dinner and then be his guest at his radio show. Younger readers of this book may not be aware that Bob Hope was then a megastar, and even though I had met him several times before (he was a former Clevelander and often came back), this was like an invitation to dine with the gods on Mount Olympus. Of course I accepted.

He also told me that Bing Crosby was doing a movie at Paramount at the same time, and I asked if I could meet him. He said it might be possible. Now in the past, particularly when I was at MGM, I was always flustered whenever I met some big star. Even with Spencer Tracy, who was awfully nice to me, all I could do was blubber. So on the plane to California I wrote down 10 things that I might say to Bing Crosby, things other than "Hello, how are you . . . good-bye." I felt I had some pretty snappy comebacks for just about any situation, and memorized them.

We landed in Los Angeles. The girl, her family, and our sponsor from Coca-Cola were taken by one limousine to one of the better hotels in Hollywood, and another limousine drove me to Bob Hope's home.

In anticipation of dinner with the great man, I had bought a whole new outfit in Cleveland, from socks to breast-pocket hankie, and now changed into it just before we landed.

I even sat in the limo with my legs straight out, so I wouldn't wrinkle the pants, all the way to what I envisioned as Valhalla. At the front door I was escorted in and introduced to the lovely Mrs. Hope, who excused herself to see about dinner. A servant offered me a cocktail, but I didn't want to sit down and mess up my spiffy ensemble.

Then in walked Bob Hope, fresh off his golf course, attired in slacks and a sport shirt.

"Where's that alleged comic from Cleveland?" he asked, then he looked me up and down and said, "Did somebody tell you I died? Take off your coat and relax."

Dinner was wonderful, but only the beginning of a great evening. We—the little girl, her family, and our Coca-Cola sponsor—were driven to the radio show. They sat in the first row, and Hope had me stand in the wings. At one point in his warm-up he said he wanted to introduce a friend of his, and I almost fell over when he said "Linn Sheldon, from Cleveland, Ohio."

I came out, flabbergasted. By now I had had many years in show business, but being introduced by Bob Hope was a once-in-a-lifetime thing. I laid some one-liners on him.

"How d'ya like that?" said Hope, "you ask a friend out here and he gets the laughs!"

The audience loved it, and so did I.

Then he said, "So why don't you introduce the man who brought you all out here, the man from Coca-Cola?"

I was so excited it was hard enough for me to remember my own name, and now I drew a blank on the name of my friend and sponsor. I stammered and said, "Mr. Coca-Cola."

He stood up, laughing. He understood.

We were invited back to Mr. Hope's home after the show, and we spent the evening in what might be called the recreation room—but it was unlike any rec room I had ever seen. It was more like a museum. The ceiling was 12 feet high—or higher—and had been fashioned from propellers from planes flown in World War II and signed by crew members. The walls were lined with glass-enclosed shelves: one was filled with honorary police badges; another with honorary firefighter badges; others with mementos from movies and radio shows; there were gifts from royalty throughout the world. Hanging along the perimeter of the ceiling was a collection of the most beautiful Indian headdresses I have ever seen, presented to him by tribes who had named him honorary chief.

There were two pool tables in the room, and let me tell you (as he might say), if you ever get a chance to play pool with him, don't do it for money.

At 6:30 the next morning we had to be at Paramount Studios for the *Son of Paleface* filming. We were all keyed up, I as much as the girl, her parents, or anyone else within about 50 miles. I fact, I was so keyed up I suddenly had to find the men's room—fast. I asked one of the security guards where the nearest restroom was. He pointed and said through the commissary.

I went in there, but I didn't see a sign that said GENTS or even GENTLEMEN. So I walked up behind a guy who was having breakfast at the counter, tapped him on the shoulder, and said "Sir, if I don't get to a restroom within the next 10 seconds, we're all going to be on the six o'clock news."

He said, "It's right over there."

I turned, started toward the door, did a massive double take when I realized who it was, and said in a high voice: "Thank you, Mr. Crosby."

So much for snappy, well-rehearsed comebacks.

The role that inspired Barnaby: Linn as "Og, the Leprechaun" in *Finian's Rainbow. 1940s.* (Cleveland Press Collection, CSU Archives)

Linn performing in the stage play *Desert Song*, at Public Hall. *1940s* (Cleveland Press Collection, CSU Archives)

A still from the Cleveland Play House production of William Saroyan's *Time of Your Life*. Linn is on the right, crouching. *1945* (Author's collection)

Linn and Vivian, in a WEWS-TV show called *The Sheldons*. *1940s.* (Cleveland Press Collection, CSU Archives)

Linn as Uncle Leslie. The door to the WEWS studio was always open because there was no air conditioning. *1948* (Cleveland Press Collection, CSU Archives)

Publicity shot for *Big Wheels*—note the wheels on Linn's shirt. *Early 1950s.* (Cleveland Press Collection, CSU Archives)

A still from a 90-minute play, *Everyman*, filmed in Cleveland and aired by Westinghouse nationwide. *1955 or 1966.* (Cleveland Press Collection, CSU Archives)

Barnaby in the Enchanted Forest. *1960s* (Courtesy Cleveland Press Collection, CSU Archives)

Sometimes Barnaby would excuse himself from the show to be replaced by another character. *Early 1960s.* (Cleveland Press Collection, CSU Archives)

Promo shot: *Barnaby* pre-empted for an afternoon World Series game. *1954* (Cleveland Press Collection, CSU Archives)

KYW (later WKYC-TV) "family photo," including Mike Douglas, "Jerry G" Bishop, Barnaby, Carl Stern, Clay Conroy ("Woodrow the Woodsman"), Jim Runyon, and Dick Goddard. *1964 or 1965* (Cleveland Press Collection, CSU Archives)

Barnaby and Longjohn, the invisible parrot, on the set at Channel 3. *1963.* (Cleveland Press Collection, CSU Archives)

Barnaby with Big Wilson and a star from the ice show at the Cleveland Arena. *Early 1960s.* (Cleveland Press Collection, CSU Archives)

Barnaby would often be asked to host visiting shows like the Ringling Brothers circus. This pose was shot at Richfield Coliseum. *1970s.* (Cleveland Press Collection, CSU Archives)

Barnaby promotional photo advertising the annual Cleveland Boat Show. *Early 1960s.* (Cleveland Press Collection, CSU Archives)

Barnaby with his baritone ukulele. *1960s* (Cleveland Press Collection, CSU Archives)

Barnaby (holding young fan) with (from left) Woodrow the Woodsman, Jim Ranyan, and Dick Goddard. *1963 or 1964.* (Cleveland Press Collection, CSU Archives)

Barnaby (right) and Mike Douglas (left), with McDonald's restaurants representative Bernard Streeter. Linn was a top commercial spokesman for the burger chain. *1960s.* (Cleveland Press Collection, CSU Archives)

Promo shot from the *Sportsman's Show* at Public Hall. Linn emceed the show for ten years. *1970s.* (Cleveland Press Collection, CSU Archives)

Linn in cowboy garb with his horse, "Duchess." *1978* (Author's collection)

Linn with an oversized photo outside the AC Color Lab on Superior Avenue. The photo is a favorite of Linn's, taken during a public appearance at the Sportsman's Show. *Late 1970s.* (Author's collection)

The Barnaby Years

Now we come to that pivotal point in my life when I first walk in front of a television camera as Barnaby, the character I would play on television for 32 years. I did not know it at the time, but I had spent my entire life preparing for the part. And now when I look back on it, I wonder if all those times I thought I was creating Barnaby in my image, Barnaby was really re-creating me in his.

I wonder.

Barnaby is a great success. The show is carried live over a number of Westinghouse stations, a very big deal in those early days of television. Barnaby helps open the Seattle World's Fair; almost drowns wading ashore from the Mayflower II at Plymouth Harbor; leads a huge parade of invisible pets; does a documentary about America that is translated into 50 languages and shown in 102 countries; helps a couple of cowboys win a bet; and gets whacked over the head by a 10-year-old kid with a ketchup bottle in a Baltimore grocery store.

I have my own adventures, too. I set fire to myself while drinking in a Texas bar with Robert Mitchum; do a stand-up routine at gunpoint; get trapped in quicksand; make a liar out of the so-called psychic Jeanne Dixon; and keep telling myself that my addiction to alcohol is really more of a divine right. I am, after all, a star, right?

But life is not all sweetness. My drinking spins out of control. Finally, I consent to some psychiatric help, and begin to understand what and who Barnaby really is.

17.

I hope I haven't given the impression that my life was more fun and games than trial and tribulation. There was, of course, a great deal of both. My whole childhood, it seems to me now, was itself a long and difficult trial, chock full of tribulations. Certainly being alone and on my own for so much of my childhood was bound to have a considerable impact later on.

In fact, it took a number of years, three psychiatrists, and some hospital time before I could sort out just how great that impact was.

Don't get me wrong. I don't blame my drinking, for example, on a misspent youth. I know that alcoholism is something you are born with and will take to the grave—an early one if you don't control it. I also know that whatever the cause of my problems, I (just like everyone else with their problems) am responsible for the ways I handle them.

So much for sermonizing.

As I say, I went to three psychiatrists. Two of them actually fell asleep on me. I don't know if I blame them.

I had gone to them because my personal life was going to hell, fast. Here I was with an absolutely beautiful wife, three wonderful kids, a great career, and a brilliant future, and I was drinking myself to death. Go figure.

At first I was afraid to see a psychiatrist, for fear of what I might learn about myself. On top of that, my career was chugging along nicely, and whatever I did seemed to get rave reviews. When I did the musical *Of Thee I Sing* at Cain Park, for instance, I played the role done by Victor Moore in the original Broadway production. William McDermott, the theater critic for the *Plain Dealer*, wrote, "I asked Mr. Sheldon if he had ever seen Victor Moore play the part. He said he had not. It's too bad Victor Moore never saw him."

So there I am, torn apart with booze and an inexplicable sadness inside, but singing and dancing my way to ever greater success. I was the lost and found department, all at once.

Let me tell you how bad things got. At one point I was so depressed and so drunk I had to be rushed to a hospital. There they gave me some sodium amytal. It was a mistake.

Sodium amytal, I discovered, was wonderful. Let's put it this way: once it hits you, if someone told you your house was on fire, you would say, "Oh, I bet it's a beautiful fire, can we go watch?"

I also discovered that when you take sodium amytal and drink booze on top of it, you reach the highest of the highs. Life is absolutely splendid, and you can do no wrong. So I began faking emergencies just so I would be taken to a hospital, where I could get more sodium amytal. After a time I was able to find a doctor who prescribed it in pill form. Now I could walk free, my happiness at the ready in a prescription bottle in my pocket.

At about three o'clock one morning, high on booze and pills, I collapsed in the street, gasping for breath. The cops came along and got me to a hospital, where doctors had to perform an emergency tracheotomy. A couple of days later, my neck still bandaged, I snuck out of the hospital and had a few drinks at a nearby bar.

So it was little wonder that my wife and others who cared about me kept after me until I finally made an appointment to see a psychiatrist. I was petrified. What—or whom—would we find when he unplugged my unconscious mind?

I danced around all the important issues for a long time, while the psychiatrist did his best to nudge me deeper into myself. He even did hypnosis. But nothing seemed to take away that gnawing feeling of despair.

Lord knows the good doctor, and he was a good one, tried hard enough, but nothing seemed to even slow down my drinking. The only thing that did cause me to stop was that one night in the wee hours of the morning I was high on booze, sodium amytal, and hair tonic at the Auditorium Hotel, and I looked out the window and saw all kinds of animals—zebras, giraffes, elephants. Good God! Delirium tremens.

That landed me in a hospital, which paved the way for the psychiatrist at last to deal with me in a relatively sober, stabilized situation. We began to make headway, and while at times things got terribly emotional, much of it was fascinating.

Eventually it became apparent that my biggest problem had nothing to do with sex, did not involve my hating my parents or siblings or any of the usual Freudian cliches. Instead it had everything to do with my ability to shift from one personality to another at a moment's notice, an ability I had developed as a child as a means for survival. In order to have a meal and roof over my head for a night or two, or to con a nickel from someone for a doughnut, I knew I had to be liked, and very quickly I figured out how to be liked by a lot of different people. I would, in effect, become whatever they wanted me to be—cute, funny, plaintive, entertaining. Entertaining! That was the ticket to survival, all right, and by the time I was seven years old I was a very good entertainer. I could be all knotted up, and often was, but when I needed something, I could usually get it by pretending to be something or somebody that I really was not.

One of the tests my doctor gave me was a personality profile developed by psychiatrists at the Mayo Clinic. When my doctor sent them the results for analysis, they called him and said they would love to have me come to Minnesota for two months, all expenses paid, to examine me further. In a perverse sort of way, I guess, I was very proud of that, but I was also much too busy with my career and family to go there.

The problem was, while I knew very well I could shift personality gears, I never really understood its importance in my life, and I never knew quite what to make of it. Not, that is, until the doctor and I worked it out. It's important to understand that this ability to shift from one personality to another was not psychotic. I was always aware that I was Linn Sheldon, no matter what I acted like. That was what fascinated the Minnesota doctors—that I could so easily swing from personality to personality without being psychotic.

Why is all this pertinent?

I returned to my television/acting career after my stint in the hospital, but after several months I found myself playing the character of Barnaby. And, lo and behold, when I was Barnaby the inner me could and did come together with the artist me. Now it was right and even joyful for me to be, through Barnaby, anyone I wanted to be.

So you see, it was Barnaby who set me free.

18.

Barnaby says hello . . .

Early in my television career I did a live interview show each day at noon on Channel 3 in Cleveland. Among a great many well- and not-so-well-known people I interviewed was the psychic who allegedly predicted President Kennedy's assassination, Jeanne Dixon.

In kinder words than these, I let her and my audience know I thought her predictions were more psychotic than psychic.

Undaunted, she asked me a series of questions: what day and in what year was I born . . . what time . . . my mother's maiden name . . . you know, the usual seeress stuff.

The fact is, I lost interest in her and her act very quickly, and when she left the set I didn't give her another thought. Not until a few weeks later, anyhow, when I received a letter from her.

It was her "reading" of me, based on what I had told her on the show.

"Lynn Sheldon," she pronounced, "will marry a tall, Nordic man and move to his country."

With one swing of the bat she gets three strikes: I have never met a Nordic man I'd be willing to marry (whiff). I never moved out of the country (whiff). I am a boy L-i-n-n, not a girl L-y-n-n (WHIFF!).

Some psychic.

* * *

Over the years I played a lot of roles on stage, in television, and in nightclubs. One of the roles I'm proudest of was back in the mid-1950s in a play performed live as part of the Westinghouse network series. (The series emerged later as *Playhouse 90*.) I was given the title role in *Everyman*, a tremendous play about a man who trades his soul to the devil for wealth, pretty girls, and everything else he'd always dreamed about. Of course, when the time comes for him to actually give his soul to Satan, he reneges and tries to get out of it.

Poor Everyman. I know just how he felt.

I also played the part of Og in a nightclub version of *Finian's Rainbow*. Og was a leprechaun who wanted to be mortal and went around saying (and singing) "When I'm not near the girl I love, I love the girl I'm near."

Like Og, Barnaby was a leprechaun. He loved nature, music, and all the other arts, and was infinitely curious. He would go to the ends of the earth—literally—to find an answer to a question.

For example: Why are blue jeans called blue jeans?

Barnaby's search for the answer to such a question might take minutes or hours—even spread out over several shows. It was like taking a trip through a world so filled with wonder . . . back in time . . . ahead in space . . . in your backyard. To find the blue jeans answer, Barnaby, using all kinds of visuals, would talk about how in long-ago days, before cars and trucks and TVs and such, people had to know how to take care of themselves. They had to grow their own food, build their own houses, take care of their children. It was only natural that in certain places unique natural resources and talents would arise, and a great expertise would develop. Groups of villagers would put that expertise to work to manufacture things that could be traded or sold to people in distant cities.

So it was in Genoa, Italy, where craftspeople produced a very unusual and very tough fabric using a locally grown fiber. No less a person than the English king Henry VIII heard about the cloth and ordered substantial quantities to make clothes. The only problem, he felt, was that the fabric's light beige color showed every spot of dirt.

So he had it dyed blue.

In England the fabric became known as "blue gens."

And you always thought blue jeans were as American as apple pie, didn't you?

* * *

What I tried to do was to make important things really interesting to young minds. The blue jeans story, for example, contained solid bits of information about how manufacturing came about; how societies worked together; how trade between nations worked; and, of course, how our language was built.

I urged them to read books every chance they got, and to look upon older people as those who had laid down and cleared a path for them so the kids would have an easier life. But in the end, the kids must contribute, too. They had to give, and Barnaby assured them they would.

* * *

How did Barnaby come to be?

In the late '50s, Channel 3 in Cleveland wanted to do a children's show, and to that end had acquired a bunch of cartoons—most of them Popeye—to build it around.

What they did not have was a host, so they invited about a dozen people to try out.

At the time I was hosting a morning movie show on Channel 8. I got a call from Ralph Hansen, Channel 3's program director, asking me to try out. He happened to mention that because of the Popeye angle, everyone who was auditioning was showing up in a sailor suit. But since the Popeye cartoons would only be part of the half-hour show, he wondered if that was the right approach.

It occurred to me that the Og character might be about right, so I showed up with the wax ears, straw hat, and all, and brought my baritone ukulele along as well.

I did an old English music hall classic called "Albert and the Lion," sang a few songs, and ad-libbed with a bunch of props: hats, a baseball glove, a lightbulb, and other stuff the Channel 3 people had thrown into a box.

They hired me on the spot.

I was not on contract with Channel 8, so that was not a problem for them or me. I did, however, have an agent. He was DeArv Barton of Music Corporation of America (MCA), one of the straightest, smartest, and kindest men I have ever known. In fact, there is no doubt in my mind that had I followed his advice and done all he said, I would have had great national success as an entertainer.

But there was this bartender I knew who depended on my business to feed his four hungry kids . . .

Anyhow, DeArv negotiated the contract, and Barnaby was off and running.

* * *

The Barnaby name was itself a happy accident, one of those spur-of-the-moment things that as much as anything else separates live television from videotape. If you could not do things on the fly, you wouldn't last five minutes in live TV. When the day of the first show came, I didn't yet have the slightest idea of what to call my new self. We had picked out a theme for the show, "The Clear Fountain." We had a little wooded set. And we had some puppet characters.

But no name for me.

Now the theme was playing, we were live, and I said to a stagehand named Bill Yeanert, "I don't have a name."

"My dog's name is Barnaby," he said.

"That'll do," I said.

I walked out and said: "Hi. I'm Barnaby."

* * *

We were still in the days of black-and-white television, of course, but the Barnaby in front of the camera was a very colorful character.

It took about an hour to apply the makeup. First came the wax ears. I made them by applying something called dermawax to each ear, then twisting and pulling it until they were maybe two inches longer than my real ears and looked very leprechaunish, to coin a word.

Then I would cover my eyebrows with white makeup and cover that with flesh-colored grease paint. Then I would use an eyebrow pencil to make the eyebrows very arched and high, halfway up the forehead. My cheeks and part of my chin were slightly rouged

I wore a shirt with a high starched collar, a string tie, a green coat with gold buttons, dark green trousers, and, to top it off, a flat straw hat. A rather dilapidated hat. A hat with great panache, if I do say so myself.

It was easy to get into character, once the costume and makeup were on. I could be anyone I felt like being. I could be Oriental. I could be old or young. I could sing, I could dance. Such was the power and privilege of being a leprechaun.

That was the fun of it, and the fact that Barnaby wasn't the same thing all the time had a lot to do with his popularity. He always looked the same, but he could and would take on any characterization that came to his mind.

Barnaby, in short, lived by his wits.

And to this day, I believe that he learned to do that as an itinerant kid in Norwalk, Ohio, many years before.

* * *

As weeks, months, and then years passed, other characters came to life to help Barnaby.

Each day I would write down some basic ideas for what I would do during the hour. As often as not, what I thought would fill 60 minutes would last maybe 40 or 50 minutes, and I would have to wing it for the rest of the hour.

To help out, the stagehands had placed a big, old steamer trunk on the set, and kept it filled with all kinds of props—common items like a salt and pepper shaker, a hat, an old shoe, a kazoo, lamp shade, book, telephone. I never knew what I would pull out of that old trunk.

One day I reached in, and out came an empty birdcage. I set it down, not really sure what I would do with it. I turned my back, and although I had never done ventriloquism, I gargled the word "hello," and said in Barnaby's voice, "Did I hear someone talk?"

And the voice said, "Hello, my name is Longjohn. I'm the world's only invisible parrot" and we took off from there.

I thought it was something I would do just for that day, but very soon we began to get letters from kids who said they saw the parrot. Some even drew pictures of him.

Longjohn became my foil. I could use him to set up just about any situation. He was a little devil who took advantage of everything, but he was a charming devil. The audience loved him, and he very nearly stole the show from Barnaby.

Because so many kids wrote about their own invisible pets, it occurred to me that there should be a parade down Euclid Avenue, downtown Cleveland's main street, with children and their invisible animals.

Mayor Ralph Locher said he would sign the parade permit, and we worked out the details with the Cleveland Police Department to have it on a Saturday morning. I was even able to get my friend, the actor Dennis Weaver, who played Chester on the incredibly popular *Gunsmoke*, to be parade marshal, and we lined up a couple of convertibles and several high school marching bands.

None of us had the slightest idea if anyone would show up—we thought several hundred would be really great—but we took a deep breath and on the show invited any kid who had an invisible pet to join the parade.

Saturday morning came, and it was a beautiful day. The band played, and Dennis Weaver drove off in one convertible, Longjohn (in his cage) and I in another.

Behind us walked no fewer than 8,000 kids with their invisible dogs and cats, horses, tigers, anteaters—every imaginable animal. One kid had a huge aluminum chain his father had welded in a circle as the leash for an invisible elephant. Behind him walked a second boy carrying a huge bag of invisible peanuts for the invisible elephant.

We awarded prizes for the most imaginative entries. The winner was a little Conestoga wagon fitted over a tricycle. One boy sat inside and pedaled while another sat up front holding balsa wood reins to guide the invisible team of oxen.

It was an absolutely glorious day for the kids, their families, all the invisible animals, and me.

Later that night, as we celebrated our success with a few drinks at the old Hollenden Hotel, Longjohn confided in me that he thought the event was one of his better ideas.

* * *

Several days before the big parade, I got a call from the father of one of our viewers.

"What's all this stuff about invisible pets?" he asked. There was an angry tilt to his tone.

I told him that most kids at one time or another had an invisible friend or pet who was not only a dear friend, but who helped them work their way through the puzzlements of childhood.

It turned out he was mad because his son had an invisible giraffe, but he was lost and his kid couldn't find him. I told him to tell the kid that the giraffe was in the attic, but he'd already told him to look in the attic and every other room in the house.

"Well, tell him the giraffe is out on the front lawn."

"I told him that. In fact I told him the lawn was full of giraffes, but he told me none of them were his."

I don't recall how that conversation ended. But about two weeks after the parade I was at Pat Joyce's Tavern, pondering the foibles of the world, when in came Long-john.

The giraffe was with him.

* * *

For the first two years of the show, Barnaby simply came on the air and got busy doing the things he did.

That worked well enough, but the time came to establish some kind of signature piece to open each show.

Now, Cleveland is rimmed by what is justly called the "Emerald Necklace," an exquisite series of public parks. Just the place to film an elf in his natural environment.

So Don Rumbaugh, the director/camera man, and I drove to the nearest park. I was in full costume—dark green coat with the tail wired to stick out, shirt with a wide, Dickensian stand-up collar, brown knickers, big bow tie, straw hat—and fully made up with the long ears, rouged cheeks, and arched eyebrows. We scouted around until we found the perfect area for an elf to be filmed coming through the woods. Then Rumbaugh had to go back to the car to get something.

So there I was, a six-foot elf, alone at the edge of the woods. I sat down on the ground, cross-legged, and lit a cigarette.

There was a open area right nearby, and pretty soon along came a park maintenance man on a tractor, pulling a series of lawn mowers behind him.

He happened to glance my way, and even 75 feet away, I could see him do a serious double take. He stopped the tractor, sat there a moment, then got down. He started walking toward me, slowly. Then he kind of walked sideways, the way you do when you think you might want to make a quick getaway. He looked at me. I looked at him.

"Hi," he said. "Uh, what are you doing here?"

"I'm making a movie," I answered.

"Really? Who's in the movie with you?"

"Bugs Bunny."

"Oh," he said. "I like Bugs Bunny . . ." and he just turned, headed back to his tractor, and took off.

Rumbaugh came back a few minutes later. We had a good laugh about the whole thing, then got busy filming the new opening segment. About five minutes later the cops came, looking for the crazy man who thought he was a woodland elf.

Or maybe an autograph from Bugs Bunny.

19.

The mark of a truly elegant lady is that she is always elegant without ever trying to be.

Such was Marjorie, my third wife.

When I first saw her—it was at a luncheon at the Hollenden Hotel for some charitable cause—I understood how a moth must feel when he sees his first flame. I went to her table and struck up a conversation with her and her friend. The talk was casual and pleasant, and before the luncheon was over I had asked her if she would go out to dinner with me sometime. She said yes, and gave me her phone number.

I called her that night.

She laughed, surprised that I would call her so soon, but agreed to meet me at a French restaurant near Chagrin Falls.

I pulled in to the parking lot and, unaware of it, parked my car next to hers.

We had a superb candlelight dinner with all the right wines. We talked long into the evening. When we left the restaurant, we were each aware that something important was under way, and I walked her to her car.

She got in. The window was open, and I leaned down and kissed her. Even her kiss was elegant. She turned on the ignition and drove away.

I turned around and walked right into the side of my car.

* * *

Ever so gently, Marjorie guided me to and through a level of society that I had never been privy to. To some of them I was and would always be someone only slightly above a street entertainer. Amusing, perhaps, but, rally, one of those common theatah people, dontcha know.

Marjorie held that kind of snobbery in as much disdain as I did, even though it was never directed at her. She knew perfectly well that in the highest level of society there are about the same percentages of worthy and unworthy people as there are at the lowest level.

I don't recall her ever telling me specifically what to do socially, or specifically how to dress better than I had been accustomed to dressing. She guided more by example, by being her elegant self. I watched, and learned, and I liked it. On the surface, at least, I had become a better person.

One year (and only one year) I was actually listed in Cleveland's social registry, the Blue Book. I had come a long way from the streets of Norwalk, I thought.

But that was on the outside. On the inside I was still a mess—insecure, frightened by life, and drinking more and more.

Like my other wives, Marjorie tried her best, and I failed. After two years, she filed for divorce, and I was alone again.

Not entirely, though. There was still Barnaby, his invisible parrot Longjohn, and a whole lot of kids who believed in both of them.

20.

In time word got out that Barnaby lived in a certain Cleveland suburb, and if you rang the bell he might even come to the door. Most of the time that was just fine with me. Not all that many people came by, and when they did it was usually a nice, gentle stroke to my ego. I even kept a stack of publicity photos of Barnaby on a table at the door, and I was happy to sign them and give them to kids who came by.

There were times, however, when it was not just fine with me. Like the time a little girl appeared at the door with her mom and dad. She asked sweetly for my autograph, so I signed a picture and opened the screen door to give it to her.

Then her father leaned down and said to her, "Would you like to go inside and see where Barnaby lives?"

That threw me.

"Uh, I'm afraid I can't invite you inside just now," I said.

The man glared at me.

"Oh," he snarled. "We're not good enough for you, is that it?" Then he grabbed the picture from the little girl, ripped it up, threw the pieces in my face, marched his family out to their car, and drove off.

Every once in a while I wonder how that little girl turned out.

* * *

When my daughter Abby was about seven or eight, some kids—maybe five of them, all about her age—said they didn't believe Barnaby was really her father.

Undaunted, Abby told them to come with her. She led them into our house, up the stairs, and into the bathroom, where I was taking a shower.

She yanked the shower curtain back, pointed at me and said, "See? Barnaby really is my dad!" and that seemed to satisfy them.

And I didn't even have my straw hat on.

* * *

This has nothing to do with Barnaby, but everything to do with why I love children so much.

I was awakened one Christmas morning by my daughter Abby, then seven, and my son Perry, then three years old. They each held a gift box.

"We got you two presents for Christmas," announced Abby.

"I think I know what one of them is," I said.

And Perry said, "Is it the sweater or the watch?"

"The sweater," I said.

"We got you something else, too," said Abby, and the two of them walked out of the room, boxes in hand, obviously delighted that they had put one over on their old man.

* * *

The front of our home was all windows—floor to ceiling, corner to corner.

Late one night I was reading in the living room when a lightning-loaded thunderstorm kicked up, and a short time later the power went out to the whole area.

It was bedtime anyhow, and I figured it would be a while before the lights went on again, so I fumbled my way to the bathroom and took a long, hot shower. I came out, dried off, and decided I would have a last cigarette. I made my way, naked, to the living room to get the pack and lighter off the table where I had left them.

I lit up, took a deep, satisfying drag and stood there for a while, fascinated by the lights of the cars driving up and down the street in otherwise pitch dark.

And, of course, the lights came on.

I was paralyzed. What to do?

I decided to pretend I was a statue, but then I thought, statues don't smoke, so I bolted back to the bedroom and put on my pajamas and robe.

A short time later a policeman showed up at the door.

"Mr. Sheldon, we have a complaint from the lady across the street that you were exposing yourself," he said.

I explained what had happened, and he seemed relieved.

"I thought it must be something like that," he said. "When I talked to the lady I pointed out that I couldn't see into your living room from hers, and she said, 'Maybe so, but come on upstairs with me and look out my bedroom window—you can see everything.'"

The moral of this story?

People who live in glass houses shouldn't have neighbors.

21.

One of the biggest laughs I ever got really hurt. I had been invited to appear at one of the big ice-skating revues at the Coliseum, a huge sports arena between Cleveland and Akron that is no more.

It would be a simple enough performance. I would glide out to a microphone on a little greenery-covered island in the middle of the rink, and lip-synch a song. It was something I had done a hundred times on TV, and people seemed to love it.

The fact that I had never ice-skated before didn't seem to worry anyone but me, since they would have two guys who could skate escort me to my little island.

Once on the island and in position, I would tip my straw hat as a cue to the sound man—in a booth high above the ice—to start the record that I would lip-synch to.

I was given a nice big introduction over the public address system, my two escorts grabbed me by the elbows, and we headed toward Fantasy Island.

But not, as I had expected, nice and slowly.

Fast. Very fast. Never having been on ice before, I estimated our speed at about Mach 2. Maybe even Mach 3.

About 20 feet before we got to the island, they let me go, assuming I would be able to manage. How wrong they were.

I did the greatest imitation of a windmill ever seen, waving my arms wildly. Then BANG, I hit a patch of that greenery and skidded to a stop. To punctuate the whole thing I whacked my head on the microphone.

The audience assumed it was all part of the act, and they applauded wildly. I took a very slow and painful bow, when what I really wanted to do was find a gun and wipe out anyone who had anything to do with that show.

I had left my gun at home, however, so I reconfigured my aching bones into the coolest Mr. Showman pose I could muster and tipped my hat to cue the sound man.

What filled the Coliseum was not the upbeat music I expected, but the awful wailing of a sick cow. The sound man's turntable was acting up.

Imagine. Lip-synching a sick animal. I was so furious, and I hurt so much I still don't remember how I finally got through the act.

But I do know that the audience gave me a standing ovation.

The show's promoters loved it, too.

They asked me if I would do it again the next night.

22.

I'll tell you a secret: Barnaby wears a toupee.

So do I.

When Barnaby was on Channel 3 in Cleveland, the station was part of the Westinghouse network, and the network carried the show in other markets. Baltimore among them. I will never forget Baltimore.

It came to pass that, on behalf of our sponsor, Kellogg's, I would make a series of personal appearances at a number of Kroger grocery stores in Baltimore. The company had produced a cereal box with a Barnaby mask on the back that kids could cut out and wear on Halloween.

The routine had an almost military precision to it. The exact minute I would appear at each store was promoted in newspaper ads, and I was given a security escort to make sure I got to each store on time. I was also given a bundle of miniature cereal boxes to give to children at the stores. In each store I would stand at a specific spot, usually to the right as you enter the store, and I would shake hands with the parents and their children as they passed by.

In one store in Baltimore it was a little different. They had me stand near the back of the store, so anyone would pass a great number of shelves before they got to me.

One boy—I remember his name was Phillip—came up to me. He was kind of a rugged little individual and tall for his age, which was seven or eight.

"Barnaby," he said, "do you love me?"

"Certainly I do," I said.

"Could I give you a hug?" he asked.

"Of course," said I, thinking, now that's a nice kid.

I took off my hat and leaned down. What I didn't know was that he had taken a bottle of Heinz ketchup off a shelf and had it behind him.

As I leaned down he took a full swing and broke that bottle over my head.

So I'm sitting there, stunned, in a pool of Heinz ketchup and Barnaby blood. There is pandemonium everywhere.

I could hear myself shouting, swearing.

Then I heard the mother say to me,

"That's a terrible way to talk to my son who loves you. It's not nice for a children's entertainer to swear . . ." It took 18 stitches to close the wound, and the scar is still there.

And that's why Barnaby wears a toupee.

* * *

You can still see little Phillip, if you like. He's in a freezer in a Kroger store over there in Baltimore.

I wish.

23.

Looking back, some personal appearances should have qualified me for combat pay.
There were other incidents besides the Kroger/Heinz ketchup affair. One was Barnaby Day at Cedar Point, the great amusement park in Sandusky, Ohio, west of Cleveland. I still get the shivers when I think of it.

Threats on one's life kind of come with the territory when you become a television personality. You don't have to be a star—even reporters on local newscasts will get them from time to time.

I kept getting letters from one guy who said I was bad for his children, that I had stolen them from him, and he would kill me for that. You kind of expect to get threatening letters or phone calls, and you tell your family about them and laugh bravely.

Like whistling past the cemetery.

A couple days before Barnaby Day at Cedar Point I got a telephone call and the guy said, "Barnaby?"

I said yes.

"I'm the guy who said he's going to kill you."

"How have you been?" I said, then "What are you going to use, a knife, a pistol, or are you going to bore me to death?" Brave words, racing heart.

"No," he said, "you're going to be at Cedar Point. I'll get you there. I'll use a shotgun."

And he hung up.

The more I thought about it, the more nervous I got.

This guy did not sound like he was kidding. I told my manager about it, and he called the Ohio State Patrol and the county sheriff's office. They decided if I wanted to go through with it they would pick me up in a patrol car near Sandusky, drive me to Cedar Point, and watch over me while I was there.

I didn't have to go, but the show must go on, dontcha know. (Incidentally, that phrase was not coined by an entertainer, but by the man who operated the theater and didn't want to lose the money. You can look it up.)

The day came, hot and muggy. As promised, I was driven in a patrol car and escorted to the stage of a big open-air theater. Extra police were already in front of the stage, facing the crowd. I had been assured they knew what to look for. I hoped so, because I didn't know what to look for—all I knew was that some guy said he was going to kill me.

I used what was known as a cornstick, a hand-held microphone, and walked back and forth, front and back on the stage, trying to zigzag without looking like I was trying to zigzag. But I was determined to at least be a moving target.

Could they tell I was nervous? I'm still nervous when I think about it. I can't even remember anything of what I said or did on stage.

When I was through I took my bows (bow . . . zig . . . bow . . . zag . . . bow . . . get the hell off the stage). I went straight into the patrol car. I had them stop long enough for me to thank the management and apologize for the extra trouble I had put them through—for nothing, I thought.

Don't be sorry, they said, we caught the guy.

Chills ran up and down my spine.

It turned out some lady had told a policeman about a man swearing and saying terrible things. The officer looked over and saw a man with an overcoat thrown over his shoulders and buttoned down the front, so you couldn't see his arms.

On a sweltering hot day?

The officer acted quickly; he got a fellow policeman, and the two grabbed the guy.

Under his coat was a 12-gauge shotgun. Loaded. They told me he was 15 to 18 feet away from me when they grabbed him.

I got back in the patrol car, and the sheriff asked where I wanted to go.

I said to the nearest saloon.

24.

Barnaby and I really got around.

In 1962, when I was working at Channel 3, the station sent me out to the opening of the Seattle World's Fair to film some segments to take back to Cleveland. Later on we would go to Plymouth, Massachusetts, for the recreation of the first Thanksgiving, and we did some neat western things in a beautiful place in Arizona called Wickenburg. We went down the Mississippi in a riverboat, and we spent some time at Disney World.

For all these excursions, the director/cameraman and producer went out first to set up all the shots and coordinate things with the local people we would work with. Dick Pitchki, one of those directors who doubled as cameraman, decided that I should arrive in Seattle in a helicopter and be filmed waving to someone in the restaurant atop the Fair's symbol, the 50-story-high Space Needle.

Did I tell you I am afraid of heights?

To this day I don't know what came over me, but I said to Dick, "Why not have me waving at myself?"

Everyone thought that was a splendid idea. Until I began to think about it. It seemed obvious that in order to be seen I would have to be standing in the open door of the helicopter, and when they filmed me in the restaurant I would have to be looking out another open window.

As it turned out, I didn't really mind the helicopter, but looking out that window 500 feet above the fairgrounds was really unnerving.

But all went well, and when the film was edited there was Barnaby in the helicopter, waving to Barnaby high atop the Space Needle.

There was another beautiful shot, again from the helicopter, that we used as the opening shot in that show. The camera looked down from the helicopter at more than 100 different-colored balloons as they floated gently across the fairgrounds.

I got the idea when I saw a man filling balloons with helium and tying them to strings so children could buy them and carry them around the fair. I told Dick about it, and he said, "let's do it now," and headed for the helicopter.

The winds that day were just right, blowing off Puget Sound right across the fairgrounds. Shortly he was hovering in the helicopter above as I walked up to the man with the balloons and said, "How much for the balloons?"

"A dollar each," he said.

"How much for all of them?"

"One hundred fifty dollars," he said, and I said "sold!"

This guy's eyes opened wide, like he didn't believe me. But when I handed him the money he smiled, shook my hand with one hand, and handed me all those strings with the other.

He had no clue as to what this was all about.

Then Dick waved to me from the helicopter, and I let those balloons go, and the helicopter followed them.

Every day for the two weeks we were filming there, the balloon man found out where we were shooting, approached us, and asked, "Do you need some more?"

* * *

One very bright, sunny day at the Seattle fair we were filming near the exit doors of a theater that showed one of those huge, surround-screen movies—the kind where you sit down, lean back, and almost face the ceiling. The place would become pitch black, then the film would come to life and take you on a wonderful trip to the moon.

When the film ended that day, the audience came out onto a snow-white sidewalk in the bright sunlight, and the contrast with the darkness of the theater was terrific.

Alongside the sidewalk was a series of pools, maybe 25 by 25 feet each, but only six or so inches deep. The bottom was covered with black tar, so they looked much deeper. There were no guardrails.

As the audience crowded along the sidewalk a very big, heavyset man slipped and fell into one of the pools. Aware that he did not know how to swim, he panicked and started screaming and splashing his arms like mad and yelling, "I can't swim . . . I can't swim!"

Some brave soul saw the poor guy, tore off his shirt, yelled, "I'll save you!" and did a beautiful swan dive into that six-inch-deep pool.

He stood up. The water was just over his ankles. The other guy was still sitting there, splashing away and hollering, "I can't swim! I can't swim!"

Our hero, who suffered only minor scrapes and bruises, helped the man to his feet and said, "You son of a bitch . . . I oughta take you to Puget Sound and really drown you!"

The crowd that had witnessed this little drama gave him a nice round of applause.

* * *

Someone once said that Amarillo, Texas, is so flat you can stand there on Sunday and see Monday and Tuesday coming. For a short while, when Barnaby was on only five days a week, I would head there to do a one-man comedy show for KFDA-TV.

One afternoon we were to do an outdoor commercial for Westinghouse refrigerators—live, of course. In the background were those great, flat plains, with an absolutely gorgeous sunset getting under way. Even in black and white it would be beautiful. At one point I would open the refrigerator door and wax rhapsodic about all the space it had.

We got under way, and as I opened the door a crack, I heard a noise, like a baby's rattle. Of course, it wasn't a baby, but a rattlesnake.

I shut the door, quickly, and said the only thing I could think to say:

"Folks, you can be sure if it's Westinghouse."

KFDA-TV was located on the edge of the Topsy Turvy Ranch, about a half mile off of Route 66, not far from an air force base.

It came to pass that a convoy of ammunition trucks headed for the air force base—30 or 40 of them, fully loaded—had parked between Route 66 and the station.

I had just begun my show when word filtered through that a prairie grass fire was blazing away and headed toward the trucks. If it reached them, me, my show, the station, and a good deal of the Topsy Turvy Ranch could be history.

The program manager suddenly appeared behind the camera.

"Until the fire trucks get here, keep 'em laughing!" he said in a hoarse whisper.

Whoever wrote the lyrics "Laughing on the outside . . . crying on the inside . . . " must have been watching my show that day.

The Amarillo Fire Department managed to get there in time, and luckily, other than to my nerves, no real damage was done.

* * *

Back then there was nothing between Amarillo, Texas, and Tucumcari, New Mexico, but a fence, and it's down, and one Indian sitting there waiting for the bus.

But there was great duck hunting there, and on one of those weekends I was doing shows in Amarillo a friend invited me to go with him and his buddies to a place where the ducks were in abundance.

It was in the midst of a central flyway, across one of those great Texas cattle ranches. The land was dotted with a series of potholes—waterholes, really—about 50 yards across and not at all deep. So early that morning we all piled in a truck and headed out. Each of us was dropped off at a different pothole until we were spread out over a large area.

I had no decoys, no duck calls, no dogs, no nothing. Just our thoughts and our guns. I simply sat there and waited. It was so still that you could hear someone talking a mile away, the sound skipping across the ponds.

Before long three mallards flew into my view, dropped their wings, and veered off to my right. I led them well and dropped two of them, bang, bang, with my 12-gauge pump shotgun. I pulled the straps of my waders over my shoulders and walked about 50 feet into the water, retrieved the ducks, and put them in the haversack on my back.

For the first time I noticed an oil slick on the water, and when I turned to head back my feet wouldn't move.

QUICKSAND!

I knew it instantly. It was terrifying, but luckily I had read an article about quicksand not long before that said if you remain still you'll be okay—but if you panic you're in real trouble.

So I didn't panic. I was afraid that if I fired the gun in the air the recoil might send me deeper into the muck, so I lay back, as if to float, fired the rest of my shells, and started hollering . . . HELP! . . . HELP! . . . my shouts skipping across the still waters like so many flat stones.

The others heard the shots and my shouts, ran to the truck, drove back, threw me a rope, and pulled me out of the quicksand.

I was as cold and wet as I had ever been, and covered with oil slick. It was November, after all, and the plains of Texas could get mighty cold. I stripped down to my long johns while the guys built a fire, threw a tarp over my shoulders, and gave me a pair of dry slippers. I put my boots on over those. When I felt up to it, they drove me back to my apartment.

While we were out hunting, my wife had gone to church in Amarillo and had invited some of the ladies back to the apartment for tea and cookies.

I will never know whose jaws dropped the farthest—the ladies' or mine—as I opened the door and walked straight past them like some oily, disheveled phantom, and headed for the shower. For once, I couldn't think of a thing to say.

The only one who wasn't surprised was my sweet, long-suffering wife, who by then had put up with far stranger things from me.

"I'd like you to meet my husband," she said matter of factly. "His name is Linn."

* * *

Before and even after I got into television I was booked at a lot of nightclubs by DeArv Barton, then vice president of MCA.

One of the clubs was a place in Chicago called Freddy's. I was to play there for a week, and get $500 bucks for it. Not bad pay for a struggling young comic back then.

First night, first show, I walk out and start doing my imitation of Herb Schriner, a great, back-home-in Indiana comic. Just nice, easy-going stuff.

The audience was about six guys at one table. They were tough-looking, bad-news characters, and they were not amused.

One of them kept glaring at me, giving new meaning to the phrase, "a menacing stare." I went to some blue material. He kept staring. Then I went out and out dirty.

More stares, no laughs.

One of them suddenly said, "Hey, Lou. Let's get some laughs."

Lou stood up, walked up on the stage, took a .38 pistol from a shoulder holster, and pointed it at me. I could see the bullets in the chamber. They were huge.

He cocked the gun, put it to my head, and said: "Be funny."

I got more laughs with "goo-bah-goo-goo-bah-bah-goo-goo" than from any joke I had ever told before—or since, for that matter.

I finally made it off the stage as they were applauding and roaring with laughter. I ran outside, found a pay phone nearby, called MCA, and said, "I'm leaving."

I told them what happened, and they were great about it. DeArv Barton, one of the smartest, nicest men I have ever known, even saw to it that I was paid for the whole week.

* * *

Once, in Dallas, I was taken for a ride. It was no ordinary ride.

In the early '50's I was doing a show on WFAA-TV there called *The Money Man*. It was one of the first shows ever done remote, that is, at a location outside the studio. We even had our own orchestra, led by Ray Plagenz.

The program director was a very clever guy named Jay Watson, and the show's director was Andy Sidaris, who later directed Monday Night Football and achieved fame for directing coverage of the tragedy at the Munich Olympics. Andy also later became a prolific producer of "B" movies.

One day before the show Jay gave me a handful of five-dollar bills and said, "We'll be out on Harry Hines Boulevard. I want you to hitchhike, and whoever stops, give 'em a five-dollar bill, and wing it from there."

That same five-dollar bill would be worth about 25 bucks today, by the way.

It sounded great to me, and when the camera and sound crews were ready I stood at the curb and stuck out my thumb.

Only a few seconds passed before a gorgeous Cadillac convertible, top down, came toward me and slowed to a stop. The driver was one of the most stunning women I had ever seen.

"Hi," I said. "I've got something for you," and offered her the fiver.

She ignored the gesture.

"How do you get to Delhart from here?" she asked.

That threw me.

"Just keep going north, and you'll get there," I said, although truth be known I really wasn't sure whether Delhart was north or south of there.

"Well," she said. "Why don't you jump in and show me how to get there?"

"No, really," I stammered. "You see, we're on TV right now. See that camera with the red light on it . . . ?"

"I don't care," she said. "Get in!"

At that point all I could think of to do was to turn to the camera and say, "Now back to the studio for a number by Ray Plagenz and his orchestra," and run.

* * *

The studio was nearby. I took my place on the studio set, ready to interview whatever guest was scheduled.

In walked the girl from the convertible.

"Why don't you want to go to Delhart with me?" she asked.

She was stunning, all right, and I was the stunee. Then I happened to look past her and through the window of the control room. Sidaris and Watson were in there, falling apart with laughter. That was my first clue that it was all a set-up, engineered by Watson, Sidaris, and Plagenz.

It turned out the car belonged to Ray Plagenz, and the girl was a local actress. And she was good, all right—as far as I'm concerned, much too good for any of Sidaris's "B" movies.

But I got back at them.

I kept the fiver.

* * *

One Thanksgiving Day in the mid-1960s was almost the end of Barnaby. And me.

I was working at Channel 3 in Cleveland, the NBC-owned and -operated station, and the program department decided to have Barnaby re-create the first Thanksgiving celebration on site at Plymouth, Massachusetts.

It was a very big deal. Part of the show would be shot on the Mayflower II, the board-by-board reproduction of the ship that carried the pilgrims to our shores in 1620. And 125 actors would play the parts of pilgrims and Indians. Except for the insertion of Barnaby into the scene, everything would be as historically accurate as possible.

The historians had told us, for example, that the ship had docked outside Plymouth harbor, and the first pilgrims came ashore in a small boat called the Schollop. When they were within 15 or 20 feet of land, they were so excited they jumped out of the boat and waded ashore.

I told the director I couldn't swim, but he said not to worry, it was only two feet deep there, at most.

The cameras were onshore, and I, along with two crew members in period dress, came toward them in the little boat. When the director yelled, "Jump!" I jumped.

Into about 20 feet of water.

I was close to drowning, but those two crew members saw what was happening and dragged me back in the boat. I got dried off, redid my makeup, and we reshot the scene.

This time the little boat went all the way to the beach before I jumped.

* * *

When the time came to re-create and film the first Thanksgiving feast itself, we were short on time and over budget.

The celebration took place in Plymouth in 1621. Together with the Indians the pilgrims sat outside, on logs. The food was all mixed up in wooden bowls, which were passed from one person to another. If you were the last to get the bowl, you took whatever was left there.

The structure of the show called for Barnaby to be the last to get any given bowl. So we sat there and passed the bowls, and as they were passed, the camera, on a track, would film them. There was no sound with this, so the director could talk to each person as the bowl came to him or her.

"Take out the duck," he would say, or "take out the clams . . ." or whatever.

As I remember there was no turkey at that first feast. Most of it was food from the ocean.

As one of the bowls got to me I looked in, and all that was left was a raw sea bass. I swear it was staring right at me. I hesitated. I like fish, but raw sea bass?

The director said, "Hey . . . we're short on time and out of budget—eat the damn thing!"

I took a nice bite out of that sea bass, and I smiled at the camera. It was the best acting I had ever done. The second the shooting was over I headed for the shore and returned to the deep that which came from the deep.

* * *

During the week or so we were in Plymouth I visited a big, beautiful old New England home, painted a soft yellow, with black shutters and trim.

I had been told that the owner had some toys that were actually used by pilgrim children, and I wanted to find out if we could use them in our documentary.

I was greeted by a maid, led into a lovely living room that had an exquisite concert grand piano as a kind of center piece, and told that the man of the house would be down shortly.

He was a warm, gracious man who won me over immediately with an offer of a martini. We sat and talked, and he said of course we could use the toys in our production. I asked him if I could try out that beautiful piano, and he was delighted. I played a couple of songs, then he sat down and played. He was very good.

"Now that's a great piano!" I said.

"Thank you," he said. "I made it."

His name was Baldwin, and he was the head of the Baldwin Piano Company. I don't believe I ever knew his first name.

* * *

The United States Information Agency made me an offer I couldn't refuse, and almost killed me in the bargain.

They asked if I would do a show wherein Barnaby would magically move from coast to coast and talk about the wonders and beauties of our nation. it would be translated into 50 languages and shown in 102 countries around the world.

What an honor! What a pay check! How could I refuse?

The opening of the show made use of special effects —crude, compared with today's effects, maybe, but state of the art for television in the 1960's. The object was to show a whole lot of Barnabys walking across the country, but through a mist. The mist would vanish to reveal Barnaby in one part of the country or another, talking perhaps to a farmer or a kid, or just describing the spectacular scope and scape of the land.

To accomplish this a monstrous, tubular-shaped construction, its inside covered with mirrors, was lowered over me. I stood on a metal stand about a foot high. The stand itself was in the middle of a rubber tub, much like a kiddie swimming pool. Then they put dry ice in the tub and poured water on it to create the mist. The camera then shot through a small opening in the mirrored wall.

Voilà! An infinity of Barnabys walking through the mist.

So here I am on top of that metal stand in the dry ice, the camera is rolling, and I am doing my best walking-in-place pantomime. It's great. The camera is filming this army of Barnabys floating in the mist . . . coming at you . . . moving away, all kinds of angles.

Well, the dry ice and water were so cold the rubber tub froze and shattered into little pieces, like so many potato chips, and the water crept out from under the tube I was in and headed across the studio floor.

Much more then than now, television studios were criss-crossed with wires and electrical connections.

What we have now is Barnaby standing on a metal riser and water heading toward some of those exposed switches. I wasn't fully aware of the danger until I heard the director shout over the PA system:

"For God's sake, cut the electricity! He'll fry if that water hits that switch!"

What I then shouted was not translatable into any of the 50 languages the show was broadcast in.

* * *

One of the people I met on the U.S. Information Agency show was Jim Henson, who created the Muppets. He was a wonderful man and a delight to work with.

In the show, Barnaby and a seven-year-old boy named Billy Brown would travel to different parts of the U.S. and every once in a while would run across Ralph and Kermit the Frog and talk with them about how wonderful it is to live in such a beautiful country.

The first night we worked together, Henson was short on money and borrowed $25. He paid me back with a check the next day.

I should've saved the check. It would have been a nice memento to show my grandchildren, and proof that I had worked with one of the true legends in the field of entertainment.

* * *

I was always pleased when anyone asked for my autograph, and always happy to sign.

If a grown-up asked for it, it was often accompanied by ". . . I don't watch your show, but could you make it out to my daughter Maggie?" and I would wonder, if they didn't watch the show, how did they know who I was?

Kids were different. They were right up front about autographs, and everything else for that matter. Not that I don't like grown-ups. They are some of my best friends.

In a career that lasted a half century, I signed thousands of autographs. But one stands out above all the others.

I was having dinner with my wife. At one point two young boys—10 or 12 years old, maybe—came over and asked for an autograph, and I said sure. We put the paper on the table next to my plate, and I signed.

A little boy—five years old, maybe—was with his mom and dad at a table nearby. He watched as I signed for the two older boys. Then his father gave him a piece of paper and a pencil and assured him it would be all right if he asked me to sign it.

When I say little, I mean just that. The top of his head was even with the top of the table, so I pulled a chair next to mine and said, "C'mon up, pal." He climbed up, perched on his knees, and set the paper next to my plate. Then without a word he took the pencil and very slowly, almost painfully, wrote something on the paper.

He looked up at me and very quietly said, "Thank you," slid the paper over to me. Then he took the pencil, climbed down from the chair, and returned to his mom and dad.

For all the autographs I have ever given, the one I'll remember forever is the one he wrote on that paper, "B I L L Y."

* * *

In the late '50s, AFTRA (the American Federation of Television and Radio Artists) went on strike against the NBC-owned and -operated station in Cleveland.

The station was on the second floor of a bank building. It fronted on one of the city's busier downtown streets, but in the back of the building a single door, lit by a bare bulb, opened to a narrow, lonely alley.

It was fall, and folks seemed to want to take a little

time off, so a strike seemed like a nice idea. Like many others, I wasn't entirely clear on what all the issues were, but then, I reasoned, that's what union leaders are for.

The meeting at which the strike vote was taken was next to a hotel. Someone suggested that we get rooms there in which to negotiate. That was the story we told our wives, anyhow, and we would stick to it. Actually, the union officials were doing all the negotiating elsewhere.

Our only official function was to picket the building. We were to have two stationed at the front entrance, and one at that dismal, lonely door in the back.

So we stayed there for several nights. We called our wives and told them we were hashing out the new rules and pay scales and such. The truth was we were playing poker, drinking a lot, and doing our best to fend off the insistent charms of some of the city's fallen doves who just happened by.

By the tenth day into the strike the novelty had gone, and the fun had worn thin. I distinctly remember one of the men, probably me, saying "we've got to settle this thing before we all die." We had drunk an ocean of booze, and a number of the people had lost a lot of money playing poker with a bellhop named Ace.

Finally, word came that a settlement was in sight, but we would still have to man the picket lines until the last "T" was crossed in the new contract. We cut cards to see who would pull final picket duty. One of the guys—a young and wonderfully funny young kid named Tom—drew a deuce and went to the back door. I cut to a four and a disc jockey friend cut a five, so we went to the front door.

It was a very nasty night. The wind was blowing hard and cold, and it had begun to sleet. In spite of our heavy coats, we were quickly soaked through and very cold.

At about eight o'clock the hotel manager came out and told us it was all over, come on in and get warm. We quickly changed into dry clothes and headed for the meeting on the second floor of the station next door.

There was great joy there—people dancing and shouting and drinking.

Somewhere around midnight, about four hours after the strike had been settled, someone asked, "Where's Tom?" Tom was the kid at the back door. All alone, and miserable.

We hurried through the studio on the second floor, opened the window above the back door, and looked down. By now the sleet was worse. It was like looking down on a foggy street in London. Dead cold. Whistling wind.

There, shivering under the misty light, was our friend Tom, who later changed his first name.

"What are you doing down there, Tom?" I called. "The strike ended four hours ago!" He stared at me in disbelief, then rage, and let fly his cardboard-and-wood picket sign.

It missed me by that much—the sign that Tim Conway threw.

* * *

When NBC took over Channel 3 from Westinghouse in the '70s, I was asked what kind of special I would like to do for the approaching fall season.

I was always a great fan of the westerns—Tom Mix, Ken Maynard, Hoot Gibson, and, of course, John Wayne—so I said I'd like to do a western, and they said fine.

We settled on a location, the Ramuda Ranch in Wickenburg, Arizona, about 90 miles north of Phoenix. It was a working ranch, and simply beautiful. Wickenburg itself was, at least then, a town of about 200 people, if that. There were a few little houses, a bank, a tack shop for saddles and other ranch supplies, a feed store, a grocery store and a saloon called Antlers Bar. It had about eight stools and, depending on the day of the week, a mule and a couple of Indians.

The ranch went up the side of a mesa, and the view from the veranda of the guest house was magnificent. At night you could see the little town of Wickenburg all lit up, like a ship at sea.

The guest house was like heaven to a western fan like me. I could think of nowhere else I would rather be than right there, on that mesa, with horses, beautiful sunsets, great food, wonderful camaraderie, and, it turned out, a great movie star, Robert Mitchum.

He was a very interesting man, very knowledgeable about the entertainment world. He was a particular fan of Laurel and Hardy and W. C. Fields. Over drinks on the veranda we exchanged stories about them. We also talked over the script for the Barnaby show and what I was expected to do.

I told him I had reservations about wandering around the ranch in my Barnaby makeup, what with all those dozens of tough cowboys around. He asked if I was getting paid for it, and when I said I was he said, "In that case, go on out there and say, who cares? You're getting your money and this is what you do, and that is what they do. Then set your lips and start acting, pal."

He made me feel a lot better about the whole thing.

But early the next morning—we would start shooting at sunrise—I saw the new cowboy outfit that our producer had put together for Barnaby, and I got nervous all over again. In addition to the facial makeup (brighter than usual for the color sets of those days) and the long ears, I would wear a pink cowboy suit with a blue silk polka-dot bow tie and yellow cowboy boots.

Not only that. You've heard of a ten-gallon hat? Well, this was about a thousand-gallon straw hat, with holes to accommodate the ears, which would be stretched even longer than normal.

For the opening of the show I would come into the scene on a stagecoach. The coach was about a half mile away, and the camera was set facing the sunrise. They drove me there in a Jeep, and I felt so ridiculous I was sure I couldn't go through with it.

Sitting in the driver's seat atop the coach was a big, burly, leathery-faced cowboy, a man's man if ever there was one. On the way out the Jeep driver told me about him—a real tough dude, he said, by the name of Charlie. Charlie had bummed around as a rodeo rider, been cut up in fights, and had done any number of other things that westerns were built around.

When I got out of the Jeep, there was Charlie, looking tough and mean. He looked at me, appraised my Technicolor outfit, and said, "Boy, I'd sure like to fuck you."

I about fell down laughing. Somehow, though, the scene drove away my case of nerves, and I knew I would get along just fine.

One of the scenes we wanted to shoot involved putting me on a Las Vegas-bound passenger train that went through but did not stop at Wickenburg. The promotions people had made arrangements with the railroad to stop the train, let me climb aboard the observation car at the end of it, and be filmed waving good-bye to the camera as the train pulls away. At the same time a bunch of cowboys on horseback would be chasing the train and shooting their six-guns in the air.

The camera started rolling as the train stopped. I got on, the whistle blew twice, the train started up, and the cowboys chased and whooped and hollered and shot their guns like mad as I waved good-bye.

The conductor, who as captain of the train had a schedule to keep, wanted no part of all this nonsense. He was furious. About a mile down the track a guy was waiting for me in a Jeep. The train was to stop, I'd get off, and he'd drive me back.

But the train didn't stop. In fact, it was steadily picking up speed. I looked out and saw the Jeep, headed in the other direction.

I went into the lounge area of the observation car. The people sitting there were not expecting a cowboy with long ears, thousand-gallon hat, and yellow boots.

But then, I wasn't expecting the train to keep on going, and if I didn't get off there'd be all kinds of problems.

Have you ever wondered this: if you pull that little chain in the Pullman car will the train really stop?

Well, I did, and it did. Fast .

The conductor was ready to shoot me, and I jumped off that train as fast as I could. The Jeep had followed along, and I was able to climb in and head back to the ranch.

* * *

At the end of the film we were doing, called *Cowboy Barnaby*, I was to be at the base of the mesa. The cameras were up on top, but you couldn't see them from down below. The director would communicate with me through a bullhorn.

So I'm sitting on a horse all by myself, smoking a cigarette, wearing the pink cowboy outfit with the big, blue silk polka-dot bow tie, yellow boots, and ears sticking up through the thousand-gallon hat. I was waiting for the director to tell me to start up the mesa. At the end of the show the credits would be rolled over the scene of me and my horse slowly making our way up the hill.

Now, two guys from another ranch who had never seen me were walking their horses nearby. They were about 25 yards from me, coming around bushes and rocks and saguaro cactuses. They couldn't take their eyes off me, and couldn't say a word. Then they turned and galloped away.

I just sat there, smoking my cigarette.

Pretty soon the cowboys came back with another guy.

The first two pointed at me. The third guy looked over at me and then gave money to the first two.

They had won the bet.

* * *

One day I was sitting on the veranda having an after-dinner martini with Robert Mitchum. We talked about going down to the Antlers Bar for an after-after-dinner drink. At the time I was not married, and I thought maybe there'd be a girl down there, but I also knew that if I went with Robert Mitchum no girl would so much as look at me.

I told him I didn't want to go down because I would be looking for a lady and maybe there's two in that whole town and one would have the flu and I would lose. I said if he was there I could set fire to myself and no one would notice.

After another martini, though, he persuaded me to go down there with him.

Mitchum had a big pair of dark glasses and a big hat. The barmaid at the Antlers Bar, who was reasonably attractive, asked if we were from the Ramuda Ranch, and I told her we were. She said someone had told her Robert Mitchum was there. I said I didn't know.

She said I should tell him if he is up there and comes in to the Antlers Bar, he could have anything he wants. Then Mitchum said in a strange voice, "Does that mean a bottle of bourbon, water and three glasses, and you sitting right next to him?"

"It does," she said.

He took off his hat and glasses. The woman almost fainted, but recovered quickly.

There was an Indian sitting at the end of the bar, and she said, "Hey Wally, a round here." She came around front, and Wally set a bottle of bourbon, a bucket of ice, a pitcher of water, and three glasses on the bar in front of us.

Now there they were, sitting together, and I'm by myself, smoking and working hard on that bottle of bourbon.

Finally I couldn't stand it. I took my cigarette lighter and lit the fringes that hung from the sleeve of my leather Buffalo Bill jacket. It was burning nicely. I tapped Mitchum on the shoulder and said, "See? I'm on fire and nobody cares,"

"You know," he said. "You were right."

He poured the pitcher of water all over my sleeve and laughed.

So did the Indian.

25.

In my day I have leaned on psychiatrists for guidance and counseling. So when a psychiatrist turned to me for help I was in no position to turn him down.

"Linn," he said, "I have a patient who has clammed up on us for some time, and the only thing he will do is watch television. I know he watches your show, and he seems to like it, so I wonder if you'd be willing to go to the hospital, sit somewhere near him, and see what happens. Maybe it will jar something loose."

Frankly, the idea of going inside a mental hospital, as patient or visitor, did not appeal to me, but I agreed.

We went to the hospital, and he led me to the day room where the man was seated in front of a television set. I went in and sat in a chair near him. His eyes stayed glued to the TV, as if the answers to all his terrible problems were hidden in there.

I said nothing—just sat there, wondering if this strange encounter would ever be reported in the psychiatric journals. Suddenly he glanced over at me, then turned back to the TV. Then he looked at me again, a little longer this time. He looked a little puzzled, but I was pretty sure he recognized Barnaby—even without the pointed ears and elf makeup, but I still said nothing.

We played this game for a few more minutes, and then he stared openly at me.

"Where are you from?" he asked suddenly. I was startled.

"Norwalk," I answered.

"Norwalk?" he said. "Barnaby comes from Norwalk. Do you know Barnaby?"

"I am Barnaby," I said.

He looked at me intently, then he stood up and walked toward me. I stood up, too, not at all comfortable about what he might have in his deranged mind.

Then he put his arms around me and hugged me.

"Pal," he said. "When you're in here, you can be any-body you want to be."

Affliction, Recovery, and Retirement

Now I learn the meaning of the old song, "Time Waits for No One . . ."

After 32 years of Barnaby, and a lot of self-inflicted wear and tear on my system, I decide that it's time to hang up his straw hat.

But first there are a few things I must do that I have never done before—like having a stroke, for example. So I have one. A nasty experience, let me tell you, but softened by the attention and good humor of my children.

In time my health is mostly restored, and I decide I will do what all Ohioans seem to do when they get a little older: retire to Florida.

My life, however, has been built around entertaining others, particularly children, and enjoying my family, friends, and work in northern Ohio. Now, I am surrounded by a lot of old geezers and even more palmetto bugs. I can't wait to go back.

So I pack my belongings and head back home again, *happy to be here.*

26.

I had my last drink of alcohol—the last of many thousands—more than 20 years ago. I was at the Auditorium Hotel on St. Clair Avenue and East 6th Street in downtown Cleveland. It was named that because it was across the street from what is now known as Public Hall, a huge structure that housed two auditoriums, one that seated 10,000 people and a smaller one that seated half that many.

I'm not even sure why I had a third-floor room there that night, but I do know that all the bars in town were closed. I started to have the shakes, and a sense of terror came over me. I knew I would do almost anything to get a drink.

Then I remembered there was a large bottle of Vitalis hair tonic among the toiletries in the bathroom. I read the label and saw that it did indeed contain alcohol, so I drank it down. That slowed me down for a while, but then I got the shakes again. It was 3:30 in the morning. I walked over to the window that faced Public Hall, spread the Venetian blinds apart, and looked down into the dimly lit street.

I saw zebras and camels.

I sprang from the window and went absolutely berserk. I had the DTs. I shook and started to scream. A bellhop came running in and tried to calm me down, and someone ran down and got a shot of whiskey from the bar and gave it to me. The police were called, and I was taken to the detox wing at St. Vincent Charity Hospital. It became my home away from home for the next three weeks.

The next day the Cleveland papers had a story about the Ringling Brothers circus coming to town. Its train had arrived early in the morning, and the animals were walked up St. Clair Avenue to Public Hall. Zebras and camels among them.

* * *

There was a Dixieland band in the drawer of the stand next to my bed.

It wasn't in there all the time, only when I opened the drawer. At first I thought there was a radio in there, but the band played the same number—"Muskrat Ramble"— every time I opened it.

It was all a function of my coming off booze. I was in the alcoholic ward at St. Vincent Charity Hospital and suffering from delirium tremens—the DTs. Usually the DTs involve visual hallucinations, like I thought I'd had when the circus animals walked by, but these were audio DTs accompanied by a violent case of the shakes.

In time they go away, but it is a terrifying thing when you begin to realize your mind is playing some serious tricks on you, even when the hallucinations are as benign as hearing a Dixieland band.

From time to time I have returned to that ward to talk to the people there, trying to comfort them with the knowledge that they, too, can defeat the monster of addiction. No fancy talk, no psychobabble. I guess they listen to me because they know I've been where they are.

There was a kitchen across the hall from the ward I

was in, and in it a big refrigerator with cold cuts, cheeses, milk, and orange juice, and when you were able to get up and make a sandwich, you were encouraged to eat as much as possible.

I would always tell the patients about my experience with the audio DTs, about the things that distressed me most, and about the people who helped me find my way back. One man, on the very bed I had been in, had the shakes. I told him to hang in there, and mentioned that I had been in the same bed and had the audio DTs.

"There was a Dixieland band in the drawer of that stand there," I said, "but it's gone now." I opened the drawer to show him the band was no longer there.

"I know that," he grumbled. "Everybody knows it's in the refrigerator."

* * *

One of the men I met in the alcoholic ward was a mortician. When he was drinking, which was almost always, he would take care not to become involved in the rituals, let alone drive the hearse.

On one occasion he had slipped into a hearse to do a little private drinking when the rear door opened and his partners put the casket inside, then tapped the window and told him to take old Carl to the cemetery. He started to drive away.

Behind him were enormous limousines filled with mourning relatives and friends of the newly departed and 12 to 14 other cars behind them.

As he drove along in his drunken stupor he could not remember where the cemetery was. He made a few odd turns here and there, three or four trips down Main

Street, up and down side streets. Everyone followed him, wondering who knows what.

After about a half hour he knew he was lost, but then spotted the cemetery. He drove in and was relieved to see the open grave with mounds of dirt and plastic grass, with people standing by the green tent filled with flowers.

As the mourners moved over to the graveside, someone remarked that this sure was a lovely place, and that old Walter would rest in peace here.

It suddenly filtered through his alcoholic fog that the name of the deceased he had been driving around wasn't Walter. It was Carl. He had the wrong cemetery.

Like so many drunks, his solution was to sneak out of the cemetery, grab a cab, and get far away.

* * *

I love horses and the American West, and one of my childhood dreams was to live on a farm with horses and be a weekend cowboy.

I never did own a farm, but I did well enough that I was able to own four very fine horses, which I kept at stables in North Royalton—then a rural suburb of Cleveland.

My favorite of the four was Duchess, an exquisite sorrel quarter horse with white stockings and a blaze down her nose.

Early one Saturday morning, badly hung over from a long night of drinking, I went to see Duchess. It didn't take long before I realized I would have to get something to drink—or die. I knew the bars were not yet open, so I called a friend—also an early riser for booze—who lived about five miles away. He said to come right over, so I figured it would make a nice morning ride with Duchess.

I got to his house, tied up Duchess, and went in. It was now about 7:30. I had a few quick jolts, and began to feel all right. Then we decided to do some serious drinking.

An hour or so later I knew only two things: (1) I was plastered, and (2) I must have owned a horse, because I had my cowboy suit on. So I went outside and climbed aboard Duchess. I figured the most direct route back to the stables would be along the freeway, and somehow I guided Dutchess there.

Then I fell asleep.

The next thing I heard was a siren. I opened my eyes, and there was a police car alongside me, with the cop yelling at me to get off the horse. A long line of cars was behind us, because in my stupor my hands had flopped back and forth, which made Duchess go right or left. I had been zigzagging on horseback on a four-lane freeway.

The officer did not buy my feeble attempt at an explanation—that the horse had been eating fermented oats.

Thus I became, as far as I know, the only man in Cleveland ever to be arrested for HRWI—horseback riding while intoxicated.

27.

It was a dark and stormy night, as the cliché goes, and I was home alone at three in the morning. The snow was coming down hard. I was reading—I don't remember what—and there was a telephone on a stand next to my bed. As I read I became aware of a sinking sensation on my right side. A terrifying thought came to me, and it was all too accurate: You're having a stroke.

I reached for the telephone, dialed "O" (this was before 911 went into effect), and mumbled something to the operator, enough for her to understand the problem. The paramedics were there within minutes. (They, by the way, are among the many people we recognize and thank too little. Underpaid and overworked, they have saved millions of lives.)

They kept talking to me as they wrapped me up and strapped me to the gurney, My mind was clear enough, but now all I could do was blubber incoherently out of the left side of my mouth. As we moved outside the snow reflected the flashing red-and-blue lights atop the ambulance. Just before they lifted me in, a neighbor's head appeared in front of me.

"Are you sick?" he asked.

I thought that was kind of self-evident.

The next thing I remember is waking up several days later in a room filled with flowers. My stroke had been reported in the local newspapers and the TV and radio newscasts, and a lot of people—some of whom I knew and a lot of very kind people who knew me only through television—had sent them.

I can think of better ways to make the front pages.

As I came to I saw, through my left eye, my son, Perry, and two daughters, Lindy and Abby. They lived in different parts of the world and had come together for the first time in years. My grandchildren were there, too.

They were all crying.

I had a strange thought: if I got up and walked away, would I still be here?

Then my son noticed that I was awake. He came over and kissed me on the cheek and said, "We all love you, dad."

I was still not entirely sure if I was dead or alive.

"Is there an organist here?" I gargled.

I knew that if Perry answered something like "everything's going to be all right," I was in big trouble.

Instead he said, "Yes, we've got one waiting out in the hall, and we're paying him by the hour. So make up your mind! Go . . . or stay."

I laughed inside, and he knew it and the other kids knew it.

The crying stopped, and the healing began.

* * *

There are very few things I like about being in a hospital, but from time to time things that happen in them almost make the visit worthwhile.

A few years back I had to have an operation on my throat. The procedure, which involved going in from the outside, was a fairly serious one. When I entered the hospital I was put in a double room with a construction worker, a big, rugged individual who snored exactly as you would expect a big, rugged construction worker to snore. Loud is putting it too mildly. Explosive more approaches the fact of it. The only time I could sleep was when he was awake, and I couldn't tell him to stop it because he didn't know he was doing it.

He knew that I was in show business, and once when we both happened to be awake he asked me if I thought a lot of people in the business were funny.

"What do you mean by funny?" I asked.

"Well, you know—queer."

"Homosexuals? No, not really," I said, and that seemed to be the end of that.

That same evening visitors began to arrive, and a man I knew—a very pleasant, openly gay man—walked past our door, glanced in, continued on and then, realizing it was me, came back and stood in the doorway.

"Linn?"

"Yeah," I said.

"Oh, my God. I didn't know you were in here," he said in a lilting voice. "I came in here to see a friend of mine."

Then he came in, flowers for his friend in hand, and said, "You poor thing. I wish I could spend some time with you, but I must go see my friend. Maybe this will help."

Before I could say anything he leaned down, kissed me on the cheek and said, "Bye-bye," and tripped lightly out the door.

My roommate never snored again.

* * *

I was in the hospital for three days before the actual operation, and after the operation I had to lie very quietly for a few more days. The doctors were very emphatic that I should not laugh, yell out, or even sneeze, because any sudden movement would take all the stitches out of my neck.

This I intended to do. Follow that rule. Oh, yes!

About eleven o'clock that night the very sweet, tender voice of an 80-year-old lady down the hall came wafting our way.

"Good-bye, everybody," she wailed, "I'm slipping . . . ." Her voice quivered. "I'm finally going to see my Walter." Then a long pause, and again, "Yes, I'm going to meet my Walter. I know he's there . . . he's waiting for me. So, good-bye, everybody."

She kept this up for about 10 minutes, telling us all that for sure she would meet her Walter in the great beyond, and what a wonderful man he was, and bidding us all good-bye. Then there was silence. It was very touching and very sad, and I felt sorry for her.

The next night, about the same time, the same little voice squeaked out, "I didn't go last night, but I'm slipping fast. Now I'll see my Walter." Long pause. "And Abraham Lincoln, too. I've always wanted to meet Abraham Lincoln. Do you want me to tell anybody anything? If you do, tell me. I'm going now. Bye-bye . . ." and so on, for another 10 or 15 minutes.

The third night we heard, "I'm REALLY going tonight. That's right. I'm REALLY going tonight to see my Walter . . . "

As she said the name "Walter" an angry, booming man's voice rumbled down that sterile hall:

"Will you go ahead and die, you old son-of-a-bitch, so we can get some sleep?"

Bye-bye stitches.

* * *

I felt pretty good about being a hometown hero in the Fourth of July parade.

It was in Norwalk, Ohio, July 4, 1996. Bob Price, my best friend and one of the town's leading citizens, had asked me to take part. I was picked up at Bob's house by a man in an old, red Buick convertible, and we drove to the high school, where the parade was forming.

I had spent a little over one school year there, and I thought it might be fun to go inside and look around—especially the stage where I played the part of a consumptive Chopin.

Then I thought, maybe not—I might find a plaque that said, "Linn Sheldon slept here."

Before long, the parade got under way. I wore Barnaby's signature straw hat, and a sign on the side of the car said, "Linn Sheldon" and underneath that, "Barnaby."

It was right out of a Norman Rockwell painting of the Fourth of July in smalltown America. Marching bands in their gaudy uniforms led by pretty girls twirling batons . . . fire engines with sirens keening . . . Uncle Sam on stilts . . . policemen more comfortable walking a beat than marching in unison . . . the mayor of the town in a car courtesy of the local car dealer . . . veterans of wars from World War I to Viet Nam, some still fitting nicely in their uniforms and marching smartly, others who should have worn their civvies . . . a unicycle team. You know the rest of it. At one place and time or another in your life you've been to a parade just like it.

It was wonderful. At one point I got out of the car and walked over to the crowd along the side, just to shake hands and say hello. A lot of people recognized me, which is always nice, but I heard a number of smaller kids ask, "Daddy—who's that man with the straw hat?"

Back in the car, we moved past the old folks' home. Its denizens, many of them in wheelchairs, were lined up on the porch. The youngest looked to be about 120 years old. None of them asked, who's that man in the straw hat?

Tempus, as somebody once said, sure does fugit.

I say again, it was a wonderful time, a gentle reflection of the way things used to be in America, and might be again if we try a little harder.

About two weeks later I received a letter from the parade marshal, thanking me for taking part in the parade. With it was a check for 10 dollars. On the line at the lower left-hand corner of the check were the words: "For second place in float."

I must have qualified as a float when I was on foot, walking past the reviewing stand. That was, after all, the only time the judges saw me.

"First place in float," I learned later, went to one honoring Thomas A. Edison, who as a boy had lived a few miles away from Norwalk in the town of Milan.

If they'd seen me in that spiffy red Buick, I'll bet I would've come in first.

* * *

I have a thing about keeping my car clean. I have no idea why, I just do.

Usually I like to wash and wax it myself. Not only

does the car look better, but I feel better for having done it. Like I cleaned myself up in the process.

But there are times when I'm in a hurry, and there's a lot of mud on the car, so I head for a drive-through car wash. One of those times the phrase "haste makes waste" took on a whole new meaning for me.

I had pulled my Thunderbird into the car wash. The attendant shoved down the aerial, went through the menu of services, noted my choice, and told me to pull up to the entrance and put the gear in neutral.

I felt the conveyor catch my car, like the lurch at the beginning of a roller-coaster ride, and enjoyed watching all the soaps and sprays and lights and whistles and bells.

About halfway through the cycle the electricity in the building went out and everything came to a stop. I didn't worry about it—I knew all they had to do was throw a breaker or change a fuse and we'd be off again. It was very quiet.

Suddenly I hear a horn blasting away behind me, HONK, HONK, HONK!

Who honks in a car wash? No one, I told myself.

Then BANG! Another car whacks mine in the rear and shoves me five or six feet ahead. I'm hit to the tune of about $1,300—the trunk, tail lights, bumper. Now the electricity comes on again . . . kaplink . . . kaplink . . . kaplink . . . and my car staggers through the exit door.

I climbed out, surveyed the damage, and turned as the lady who was driving the other car approached.

"Didn't you hear me honk?" she asked.

"Didn't you see me wave you around?" I asked sarcastically. I was furious.

"Listen," said she, her voice rising in panic and confusion, "I've got to get to the hairdresser. Look how frizzy the back of my neck is."

"Frizzy on the back of your neck?" I said. "Look at the frizzy on the back of that Thunderbird." At this point I hadn't been drinking for about five years. When I called my insurance man, a nice guy and an old friend, he asked where the accident occurred. I told him it happened in a drive-through car wash.

There was a long pause.

"Uh, Linn," he stammered, "how're you coming along with, you know, your problem?"

28.

There is a time and place for everything, but Florida was neither one for me.

I hung Barnaby's straw hat up in 1990 and headed for Winter Park, Florida. After all, I was 70 years old, and because so many do, I thought there must be a law that said when you turn 70 in Ohio you go to Florida.

To frolic with other old people.

I felt like the Jimmy Durante lyrics: "Didja ever get the feeling that you wanted to go . . . that you wanted to go but you wanted to stay?"

So with some reluctance I packed a pair of white shorts, open-toed sandals, sunglasses, and my umbrella and headed south for a quiet retirement in a very nice apartment in a building on the edge of Lake Oseola.

My first night there I was excited, and I found it hard to sleep. I got out of bed, went into the kitchen, turned on the lights, and suddenly saw thousands of spots in front of my eyes. They went away quickly, and I worried about it until someone told me they weren't spots—those were palmetto bugs.

Up north we called them roaches.

* * *

I knew that I would be reasonably anonymous down in Winter Park. Barnaby never played in Florida, and while like many performers I loved the attention of the public, I also longed for privacy.

So I was surprised that as I strolled through the area on my very first day there, two old ladies walking toward me had spotted me as a celebrity—even with my sunglasses on. I heard one of them say, "I think that's him. I'm sure it is . . . go ask him."

And the other old lady came up to me and said, "Soupy Sales, right?" and asked me for an autograph.

I signed Clark Gable's name.

* * *

A few days later I was startled by a loud siren, and everyone scurried indoors. Like the palmetto bugs, I thought. Or an air raid.

In a sense, that's just what it was—an air raid. The siren was a warning that a truck was on its way to spray the area for mosquitoes. I went inside. The mosquitoes followed me in.

* * *

Now this actually happened: one day I was window shopping at the local stores, and I saw a necktie that I liked very much. I went in and told the clerk I would take it, handed him my credit card, and turned pale as he punched in the price: $100.

Pride goeth before a fall, and so did my hundred bucks. I did not have the guts to tell the man that no tie ever was, is, or will be worth a hundred simoleons to me.

I should have known better than to buy something without asking the price. There were homes around there that were simply staggering in their beauty, not to mention their cost. I was invited to tea at one of those homes.

The people there, and I mean this, didn't like the Florida sand, so they imported the sand for their beach from the Caribbean.

I didn't see any palmetto bugs in that home, but if there were any, I bet they had the family crest on their backs.

Did I mention that at the age of 70 I was the youngest person in my apartment complex?

Once or twice a week the evening ambulance would come by, and another apartment would become available. I suggested that we have a raffle to guess who would go next Tuesday. The winner would get a free cat scan, physical exam, and an overnighter at the hospital of his or her choice.

And I won.

It was at the physical that I discovered I was allergic to palmetto bugs.

So now I'm home back north, where, as Gertrude Stein would say, a roach is a roach is a roach.

29.

I first met my present wife, Laura, when I was working at Channel 61 in Cleveland. It was actually well after the death of my second wife, Vivian, when I was finally emerging from the impact, that I saw Laura. She was working in the accounting office in the station's one-story building.

Years gone by can make a mockery of youth's beauty, but not of Laura's. She is as beautiful today as she was back then, in her early twenties.

The first time I saw her I asked her out to lunch. She turned me down. A few days later I asked her out again, and she turned me down again. It was raining hard that day, so I went outside and stood by the window of the accounting office and, soaking wet, pantomimed my pleas to go out with me.

One of the other women in accounting told her, "For God's sake, Laura, talk to the talent before he gets pneumonia . . ."

She talked to me, but only to turn me down again.

A day or two later I knew she was going out to lunch with her girlfriends from work. I also knew where she hung her coat, so I went to that closet, put on her coat, and waited. When she opened the door, there I was.

"Either you go to lunch with me, or you go to lunch without your coat," I said, and that got to her. We went to lunch, and began dating regularly.

Then Kaiser decided to close the station down. I went

to Channel 3, where Barnaby was born, and not long after that signed a long-term contract to do Barnaby at Channel 43. In that shift, Laura and I drifted apart, and I wasn't to see her again until after I retired, moved to Florida, and back to Cleveland again.

* * *

Then one day I saw her walking along a sidewalk in Lakewood where, it turned out, we both now lived. That chance meeting led to a lot more meetings that were anything but chance.

Laura and I were married by the mayor of Rocky River, a mutual friend, in his home on Christmas Eve. Then we went on our honeymoon.

To Heinen's.

Heinen's is one of the finer grocery chains in northern Ohio. We went there for the simplest reason of all. We both had a craving for pizza.

We settled in a fine apartment on the shore of Lake Erie, and looked forward to all those golden years that people talk about.

The only problem with that was that I soon discovered that I had developed diabetes and, worse, lymphoma cancer. When the doctor gave us that word, it was Laura who said, "We'll lick it. Together"

And we have. Together.

Thus Laura has given me something that no one else ever could give me: the strength to endure and overcome. Pride in myself.

She made me whole.

Afterword

When I began my journey into show business, vaudeville was on its way out, but many of the great entertainers who had kept it alive for years were still around. And because they were supremely competent performers, they were as busy as ever.

One in particular was a true mentor to me. His name was Roy Atwell. In addition to convulsing theater audiences with (among other routines) a brilliantly twisted recitation of "Little Red Riding Hood," he played many film and Broadway parts. He died some years ago, but his voice lives on as the voice of Doc in Disney's *Snow White*.

I met Roy when we were in a road company of that sweet old musical, *Rosalie*. Being on the same stage with him was superb on-the-job training in timing, presence, pacing, and every other aspect of performing before an audience.

He had worked with many of the legends of legitimate theater and its illegitimate offspring, vaudeville, and was a friend of others—W. C. Fields, John Barrymore, the Marx Brothers, Eddie Cantor, Bert Lahr, Bert Wheeler, and so many more.

He was a member of the very exclusive, all-male gathering place for great stars, the Lamb's Club, and in fact lived there. Considering that the club allowed each member to have only one guest for one day each year, it was a measure of our closeness and a great thrill for me when he invited me to the club as his guest.

One story he told me there was of John Barrymore, the great Shakespearean actor, who was banned for six months for having swept his cane across the club's back bar in a drunken rage, smashing bottles, glasses, and mirror in the process. Six months to the day later he returned, cape, cane, slouched hat, and all. Someone asked him why he had been banned.

"For this!" he exclaimed, and with a sweep of his cane knocked every bottle and glass off the back bar.

Now that's what I call a grand gesture.

Back to Roy. Among the many things he taught me, this seems to be the most important, and one he stressed over and again:

Know when to get off the stage.

It is an axiom that every great performer has understood since the first caveman grunted to another "Take my wife—please . . . " and did two a day in a hole in the ground.

"No matter how many more jokes or stories you have, leave them wanting more. That way they will always invite you back," Roy would say.

I've told a lot of stories here, and I have a whole lot more to tell. But if I keep on, I'm afraid you might not invite me back.

So for now I'll just say good-bye.

And if anyone calls, tell them Barnaby says hello.

And so do I.

Postscript

Barnaby says goodbye.
(From his farewell television appearance.)

Morning, neighbor. Barnaby's the name.

I'm pleased you came along. Pull up a chair and sit down for a few minutes.

This is the last day for me here in television—Barnaby, and in television in general. I've thought so long on what I'm going to do on this program, I just said to myself finally, "Just say what comes to your mind."

Things change so much, as you certainly know. The children I've played to have grown up and had their children, and they've grown up and had children. I never thought it would go this long, that I would be on this long. And you have to ask yourself, "What does it all mean? Why have I been on and other people who come along go away?"

Maybe it's because I wasn't smart enough to go anywhere else. But I do hope that something that I might have done or said changed the manner in which television is done. If I've done that, then that's all right. Then I like that. I like the thought of it. If there are some children—or adults, really—who have read one book because I suggested it, then that's important.

Did I set a good example? I don't think so, for a while. But through the help of so many wonderful people and the help of the dear Lord, I got over it—the problems—and I think it was meant to be that way. To show that, if you try to, you can get over it—whatever the problem might be.

I'm looking forward to the new part of my life. Seventy—seventy—years old! I don't tire of new beginnings, and I hope that's something you will take with you. If you do, if something comes down, if you have to leave, if you get sick, if you have a problem, turn it around—a new beginning—and don't get tired of it, because it's fascinating.

Seems like yesterday that the group of us at WEWS—Dorothy Fuldheim, Alice Weston, Bob Dale, Paul Hodges, Gene Carroll, and myself—started this television business. And I say thanks to them. I love them all. And the stations, the people, the directors, the crews.

But the person you can't do without is you.

When I say you, I really don't know who you are. But I've always thought there was one person out there that I care for more than anybody else in the world. She's probably still there. That person would be you. There've been some nice children coming along—boys too, like my own son. And good times.

This is the little bird [pointing to Longjohn] *that we started out with by accident—Hi—he can't even talk now. I'll take him along. And I hope you'll be all right.*

And if anybody calls, tell them Barnaby says hello. And tell them I think that you are the nicest person in the whole world. Just you.